Public Safety and Security Administration

Public Safety and Security Administration

P. J. Ortmeier, Ph.D.

BUTTERWORTH
HEINEMANN

Boston   Oxford   Johannesburg   Melbourne   New Delhi   Singapore

Butterworth–Heinemann supports the efforts of American Forests and the Global ReLeaf program in its campaign for the betterment of trees, forests, and our environment.

Library of Congress Cataloging-in-Publication Data

Ortmeier, P. J.
    Public safety and security administration / P. J. Ortmeier.
        p.   cm.
    Includes bibliographical references and index.
    ISBN 0–7506–7079–7
    1. Offenses against public safety—United States.   2. Law enforcement—United States.
3. Criminal justice, Administration of—United States.   I. Title.
HV6446.O77   1998
363.2′0973—dc21   98–21489
                                                                          CIP

British Library Cataloguing-in-Publication Data
A catalogue record for this book is available from the British Library.

The publisher offers special discounts on bulk orders of this book.
For information, please contact:
Manager of Special Sales
Butterworth–Heinemann
225 Wildwood Avenue
Woburn, MA 01801-2041
Tel: 781-960-2500
Fax: 781-960-2620

For information on all Butterworth–Heinemann publications available, contact our World Wide Web home page at: http://www.bh.com

10 9 8 7 6 5 4 3 2 1

Printed in the United States of America

Contents

Preface

The protection and safety of persons and property involve many and various public agencies and private organizations. They involve, among others, entities from the criminal justice system, made up primarily of law enforcement, the courts, and corrections, as well as the fire service, private security, and environmental safety. These entities are often studied separately. For example, the business-related private security function has been viewed as distinct from public safety. However, in some states, efforts are under way to include private security, because of its protective function, under the umbrella of public safety.

In 1994, a consortium was formed in California to address common issues and training goals of public safety and security organizations. The California Public Safety Training Consortium, funded through a grant from the Community College Chancellor's Office, brought together all major identifiable private and public safety entities and instructional providers. Police, judicial, corrections, fire, environmental safety, and private security agencies and businesses as well as community colleges, public universities, and private educational institutions were represented. From the outset, members of the consortium realized that cooperation and collaboration are in the best interest of their clients, consumers, and the public.

The author suggests that the protection of persons and property is a common thread through all public safety and security entities. An interrelatedness and interdisciplinary nature are associated with these agencies and organizations. A complementary and cooperative, rather than competitive, relationship between the components of the public safety and security system enhances common protection goals.

In this book, an attempt is made to address the similarities, rather than the differences, in the administration of these entities. As such, this book addresses safety and security issues and the administration of public safety and security organizations from a more holistic and visionary perspective. The intent is to focus on the theories, concepts, practices, and problems related to the present and future of public safety and security and examine different strategies for problem solving that may be used by personnel working in the field.

This book synthesizes college-level lectures prepared, presented, and updated by the author over the past twenty years. Information from other sources also is incorporated. This book is intended to be a desktop reference work for public safety and security practitioners, managers, supervisors, and administrators. It also may be used as a textbook for courses in public safety administration, law enforcement, fire science, environmental safety, corrections administration, and security management.

Part One examines safety and security concerns, including crime, loss prevention, chemical abuse, fire and environmental safety, accidents, natural disasters, civil disturbances, and liability. Heavy emphasis is placed on the legal aspects of public safety and security, including authority, criminal law and procedure, use of force, civil liability, torts, contracts, property rights, and the role of the Constitution in a free society.

Part Two provides a brief history and overview of each component of the system of public safety and security services. It addresses the changing roles, expectations, issues, and problems encountered in each component of the system.

Part Three presents an overview of the administrative process involved in the planning, organization, management, and evaluation of public safety and security entities. Emphasis is placed on identification of consumer needs and development of strategies to meet those needs. This part of the book is intended to be generic with practical applications appropriate to any public safety or security setting.

Part Four focuses on the collateral functions of investigations, documentation and report writing, and professional career education. Emphasis is placed on the basics of civil and criminal investigations, the general principles associated with report writing, and career preparation and continuing education.

Part One

Nature and Scope of Public Safety and Security

Chapter 1

Safety and Security Concerns: Criminal

Probably no other safety or security concern creates more apprehension in people than the fear of crime. Although the crime rate began to decrease in the early 1990s, the crime rate is still high and remains a major personal, social, political, and economic issue.

Crimes may be categorized in numerous ways. One method is to classify crimes as either offenses against persons or offenses against property. Other methods distinguish violent from nonviolent crime. In this chapter, crimes are categorized according to the following types:

- Street crime
- Victimless crime
- White collar crime
- Organized crime
- Domestic crime
- Juvenile crime
- Workplace violence
- Terrorism

This chapter also explores the nature and extent of crime and theoretical causes of crime.

TYPES OF CRIME

"Street" Crime

When people think of crime, they usually think of the types of crime that fall into the street crime category. These include felony crimes such as murder, rape, robbery, aggravated assault, burglary, auto theft, grand larceny, and arson. Although most crimes are misdemeanors in nature, fictional accounts of crime fighting depicted in movies and on television focus on these felony crimes. Newspapers and other forms of mass media news programs also focus on the most heinous crimes.

The crimes on the foregoing list are included in Part I of the Uniform Crime Report (UCR), which is published annually by the Federal Bureau of Investigation (FBI). Often referred to as Index Crimes, or the leading crime indicators, they include only serious crimes against persons and property. Statistics relative to these crimes are the ones that typically appear in the news. The public's perception, therefore, is that serious street crime of a felonious nature accounts for the largest percentage of crime in the United States. However, as is explored later in this chapter, most crime in the United States is not of the serious street crime variety.

Victimless Crimes

A victimless crime may be defined as a crime in which someone other than the victim is the complainant. In other words, victimless crimes refer to offenses whereby the participants enter into the activity voluntarily. Victimless crimes include offenses relating to gambling, pornography, illegal drugs, illicit sexual behavior, public drunkenness, disorderly conduct, and vagrancy. In recent years, it has been suggested that many of these crimes be decriminalized because enforcement of laws against such activity diverts public safety resources away from more serious crime, invades the privacy of individuals, and sets the stage for corruption. Another consequence of victimless crime laws is what criminologists refer to as the *secondary criminogenic effect*. That is, enforcement of such laws may indirectly create other crimes, such as burglary whereby an addict steals to support a habit. Others would retain and strictly enforce these laws and argue that victimless crimes destroy the moral fiber of society and lead to more serious offenses.

White Collar Crime

In 1939, Edwin Sutherland coined the phrase *white collar crime* and defined it as an offense committed by a person of respectability and high social status in the course of his [or her] occupation. In 1994, James Coleman defined it as a violation of the law committed by a person or group of persons in the course of an otherwise respected and legitimate occupation or financial activity. According to these definitions, white collar crime may include the following types of criminal activity:

- Political corruption, e.g., bribery
- Illegal business practices, e.g., price fixing
- Tax evasion (as compared with tax avoidance)
- Fraud, e.g., misrepresentation of facts that leads to financial gain

- Embezzlement, e.g., theft of property or money by one to whom it is entrusted
- Economic crime and industrial espionage, e.g., computer-related crime and theft of proprietary information

White collar crime accounts for a greater total financial loss to the American people than does street crime. In addition, if deaths resulting from known, yet uncorrected, workplace safety hazards were counted, white collar crime would be responsible for a death rate higher than the nation's murder rate.

White collar crime is a national security issue. According to government sources, the greatest single threat to the security of the United States today is white collar crime in general and economic crime specifically. The U.S. Trade Commission estimates that losses due to economic crime in 1982 totaled approximately $5.5 billion. By 1995, this estimate had increased to more than $60 billion. Industrial espionage, a form of economic crime, targets intellectual property such as trade secrets, financial information, corporate tactical and strategic plans, and technology. Many foreign businesses and some foreign governments are actively involved in industrial espionage against U.S. businesses.

Organized Crime

Organized crime may be defined as the systematic engagement in illegal activities and provision of illegal services by a permanent group of individuals. It involves a continuing criminal enterprise that works to profit from illegal activities that are often in great demand. The existence of organized crime is maintained through the use of threats, force, monopoly control, and corruption. Proceeds (revenues) may be used to develop legitimate businesses to use as fronts for more illegal activity. The image of organized crime is that persons of southern European ancestry, often referred to as the Mafia or La Cosa Nostra under the direction of a "godfather," engage in organized illegal activity. However, organized crime today crosses all ethnic and cultural lines.

Organized crime is involved in narcotics, illegal gambling, loan-sharking, labor racketeering, and various other illegal activities. The beginnings of organized crime, as it is known in the United States, may be traced to Prohibition (1919 to 1933). During this period, the manufacture, distribution, and sale of alcoholic beverages in the Untied States were not only illegal but also unconstitutional. However, many people in this country continued to demand alcohol. Therefore, the alcoholic beverage industry went underground, and criminals organized to meet public demand.

Domestic Crime

In recent years, concern has grown over the nature and extent of domestic abuse in the United States. The statistics are frightening. One is more likely to be assaulted, beaten, even killed, in one's home by a loved one than anywhere else or by anyone else in society. In addition, violent crime within a family setting is often the end result of a long history of domestic conflict. In fact, in most [domestic homicide cases, the police have visited the home previously.] Domestic abuse may also manifest itself in the workplace and other areas outside the home. Domestic abuse (or violence) may be defined as follows:

> Intentionally or recklessly causing or attempting to cause bodily injury [refers to actual physical contact and battery] *OR* Placing another in reasonable apprehension of imminent serious bodily injury to himself or another [California Penal Code Section 13700(a)].

Many states have toughened laws relative to domestic abuse. In California, domestic abuse is a felony, and unlike in misdemeanor cases, a police officer may arrest for an unobserved felony if probable cause exists that the felony crime was committed. Furthermore, regardless of the intentions of the perpetrator, reasonable apprehension, or fear of injury, includes any threat as perceived by the victim.

According to the statutory provision, domestic abuse, as compared with child abuse, is defined as a crime committed against an adult or fully emancipated minor in a present or past relationship of an intimate nature. This would include a spouse, former spouse, present or former cohabitant (not roommates), persons in dating or same-sex relationships, or a person with whom the perpetrator has had a child.

Juvenile Crime

Americans have become increasingly concerned over the issue of juvenile crime. In fact, most street crimes are committed by youthful offenders. However, youthful offenders younger than 18 years are typically referred to juvenile court. The juvenile court, acting under the principle of *parens patriae* and functioning as a parent on behalf of the child, has jurisdiction over dependency and delinquency. Dependency issues arise when the child has been neglected, sexually abused, or battered. Delinquency issues arise when the child commits an act that would be a crime if it were committed by an adult.

Efforts by the justice system to deal with delinquency issues are often problematic because juvenile behavior is legally ambiguous. The role of the police officer is equally ambiguous because of the conflict between the roles of law enforcement and crime prevention.

Throughout the 1970s and 1980s, juvenile gangs became a major problem in urban as well as some suburban and rural areas. Although some gangs include adult members, membership by and large is made up of teenagers. Specific problems associated with gangs include the use, distribution, and sale of controlled substances. In fact, it is believed that illegal drug trafficking provides the economic foundation for organized gangs. Other problem areas include turf conflict, in which rival gangs, using public areas as private space, compete for the same area. Finally, a major problem in dealing with gangs involves balancing law, neighborhood practices, and the image of authority without under- or overreacting to specific incidents.

Not all gang activity is criminal in nature. Some gangs are simply informal hedonistic gangs motivated by pleasure or rebellion against authority. Other gangs are culturally or ethnically based gangs motivated by loyalty to each other and protection of the membership. The third category includes predatory or instrumental gangs, which are motivated by economic opportunity and power. This last group is the most dangerous from a public safety standpoint.

Workplace Violence

In recent years, special attention has focused on the subject of workplace violence. As a result, a new category of crime has developed. In the 1990s, the United States experienced a dramatic increase in reported workplace violence. This type of crime is categorized as employee, occupational, and attached workplace violence. Workplace violence between employees is identified as employee workplace violence (violence that stems from an employment relationship). Occupational workplace violence is violence that occurs in the workplace and results from one's occupation (violence associated with unsafe working conditions). Attached workplace violence is violence that occurs in the workplace but that stems from a relationship that exists outside the workplace.

There are no absolutes and no exact answers to the issues and problems of employee-type workplace violence. Policies and procedures, however, for preventing and/or minimizing the damage from workplace violence should be addressed. Employers may be held liable for failure to take appropriate action when symptoms of potential workplace violence occur.

Terrorism

Terrorism, in its broadest context, involves the use of violence and threats to intimidate or coerce. Terrorism may be the product of an individual or a group. Examples may include illegal activities committed by the following persons:

- Idealistic and political groups
- Economic opportunists
- "Urban" terrorists or gangs, such as predatory gangs, ethnic "turf" gangs, and economic gangs
- Career criminals
- Domestic violence perpetrators
- Pro-life, anti-abortion, pro-choice activists

- Animal rights activists
- Environmentalists

Acts of terrorism are increasing in the United States. The World Trade Center bombing in New York City and the bombing of the federal building in Oklahoma City demonstrate the catastrophic nature of domestic terrorism.

NATURE AND EXTENT OF CRIME

Crime Rates, Statistics, and Trends

In 1929, as the result of congressional action, the attorney general of the United States and the FBI were authorized to develop and implement a uniform system for the collection and dissemination of crime statistics. The system was built on the recommendations of earlier efforts by the International Association of Chiefs of Police (IACP).

The system was designed to identify major crime trends by comparing seven crimes in the Crime Index, or Part I, of the UCR. The Part I, or Index Crimes, included murder, forcible rape, robbery, aggravated assault, burglary, larceny (theft), and motor vehicle theft. In 1979, arson was added to the Index Crimes list. Other crimes, not listed in Part I, were included in Part II of the UCR. The published "crime rate" refers to the number of reported crimes per 100,000 population.

Crime data is supplied voluntarily by law enforcement agencies for inclusion in the UCR. Initially, approximately 400 agencies reported crime statistics to the FBI. By 1971, approximately 8,000 of the estimated 20,000 law enforcement agencies in the United States reported such information. In 1994, 16,313 agencies submitted crime reports. It should be noted that the law enforcement agencies that do report are able to report only crime that is reported to them by citizens and victims. The profile of the typical Index Crime–prone offender is that of a young man (approximately 14 to 24 years of age) who lives in an urban area, is a recidivist (has a criminal record), and, in most cases, has an impoverished background and is a member of a minority group.

During the Great Depression of the 1930s, the crime rate in the United States declined somewhat. During World War II the crime rate declined dramatically. Some experts suggest that this decline occurred in part because most young men in the crime-prone years were involved in the war effort. In the 1960s, the crime rate began to increase dramatically. Campus unrest, protests against the Vietnam War, riots and the "coming of age" of the postwar male babies contributed to the increase in the crime rate.

In 1991, national crime rates began to decline. By 1996, the crime rate had dropped for the fifth year in a row. Crime rates in some states declined more than 30 percent during the same 5-year period. In 1997, two of the most feared crimes, homicide and robbery, showed declines of 9 percent each during the first 6 months of the year. Overall, violent crime decreased 5 percent and property crime was down 4 percent. Factors contributing to the decline have been attributed to tougher sentences, community policing, and a decline in the number of men in the crime-prone age group.

Victimization Studies

A major criticism of the UCR is that it includes information relative to crime reports submitted to the FBI voluntarily by law enforcement agencies and that only about 80 percent (approximately 16,000) of all agencies currently report such data. In addition, police agencies are able to report only crimes that are reported to them. Therefore, in an effort to obtain more accurate information on the nature and extent of crime in the United States, the U.S. Department of Justice began funding victimization studies, or surveys, in 1972.

The major purpose of the surveys was to uncover unreported crimes and the reasons for not reporting. Initially, approximately 10,000 households and 2,000 businesses in each of several selected large cities, such as Chicago, Detroit, Los Angeles, Philadelphia, and New York, were surveyed. The victimization surveys reported twice as much overall crime than was reported in the UCR statistics, the rate of theft-related offenses being four times higher than in official records. Burglary was the most common crime. Reasons for not reporting crime included (1) the victim felt that nothing would be accomplished; (2) the incident was not serious enough for police attention; and (3) fear of reprisal. Surveys conducted in the early 1990s indicated that only about one half of all violent crime, two fifths of household crimes, and one fourth of all theft-related crimes were reported to the police.

Today, National Crime Victimization Survey (NCVS) data is collected by the U.S. Department of Justice Bureau of Justice Statistics in cooperation with the U.S. Bureau of the Census. Currently, the NCVS collects data each year from a sample of approximately 50,000 households with more than 100,000 individuals 12 years of age or older. The NCVS does not measure murder (because of the inability to question the victim), kidnapping, or crimes against commercial establishments. Crimes such as public drunkenness, drug abuse, prostitution, illegal gambling, con games, and blackmail also are excluded. Although the NCVS may be more accurate than the UCR, it is not without its critics. There is, for example, the potential for false or exaggerated reports made by victims to interviewers, and no attempt is made to validate victims' claims.

New Crime-Reporting Systems

In response to criticisms of the UCR and the NCVS, the FBI has introduced a new crime-reporting system, and the NCVS questionnaires have been redesigned. Each is geared toward providing more accurate and detailed information.

In January 1989, the FBI introduced the National Incident-Based Reporting System (NIBRS). The traditional UCR system required the summary tallying of the number of occurrences of Part I offenses as well as arrest data for Part I and Part II offenses. As an alternative to summary reporting, the new, enhanced UCR, or NIBRS, was developed to deal with the volume, diversity, and complexity of crime. The NIBRS requires more detailed reports. Agencies collect data regarding individual crime incidents and arrests and submit them in "reports" detailing each incident. This incident-based reporting provides much more complete information about crimes than does the summary statistics of the traditional UCR system.

Among the major changes introduced in NIBRS is the substitution of Part I and Part II offenses with Group A and B offenses. Whereas the existing Part I is focused on "street crimes," the new Group A is more inclusive and widens criminologic interest to "crime in the suites," such as white collar crime. Group A offenses include the following:

1. Arson
2. Assault
3. Bribery
4. Burglary, breaking and entering
5. Counterfeiting, forgery
6. Destruction, damage, vandalism of property
7. Drug and narcotic offenses
8. Embezzlement
9. Extortion, blackmail
10. Fraud
11. Gambling offenses
12. Homicide offenses
13. Kidnapping, abduction
14. Larceny, theft
15. Motor vehicle theft
16. Pornography, obscene material offenses
17. Prostitution
18. Robbery
19. Sex offenses, forcible
20. Sex offenses, nonforcible
21. Stolen property offenses
22. Weapon law violations

Detailed information is provided for each occurrence of these crimes. Included among the 52 data elements collected is information detailing the crime circumstances, offender characteristics, arrestee data, victim information, and offense and property data. Less detailed information is required for the eleven Group B offenses. The Group B offenses include the following:

1. Writing bad checks
2. Curfew violations, loitering, vagrancy

3. Disorderly conduct
4. Driving under the influence
5. Drunkenness
6. Family offenses, nonviolent
7. Liquor law violations
8. Peeping Tom offenses
9. Runaway-related offenses
10. Trespass of real property
11. All other offenses

Other new features of the NIBRS include the following:

1. New definitions of offenses (Rape, for example, in addition to cases involving force, has been expanded to include cases in which consent was not given because of temporary or permanent mental or physical incapacity.)
2. New UCR code
3. Elimination of the hierarchy rule (all crimes occurring during the same incident are recorded)
4. Introduction of a new category called *crimes against society* (This provides an additional category to complement the existing crimes against property and crimes against person and includes crimes such as gambling, prostitution, and drug sales and use.)
5. Means for differentiating attempted versus completed crimes
6. Expanded data on the victim-offender relationship

As of November 1996, ten states had been NIBRS certified and twenty states were in the process of testing the new reporting system. An additional ten states were developing plans to test the NIBRS in the future. The system is intended to be fully operational by the end of 1999.

In 1995, the NCVS redesigned its questionnaires to include more detailed information on the following:

- Interaction between victim and offender
- Victim's crime deterrence efforts
- Perceived effectiveness of crime deterrence efforts
- Bystander behavior
- Perceived alcohol and drug use by offender
- Suspected offender gang involvement

The redesigned questionnaire included changes in both the content of the survey and procedures used in data gathering, including the following:

- Additional cues to help survey participants' recall of incidents
- Questions encouraging respondents to report victimizations that they themselves may not define as crimes
- More direct questions on rape, sexual assault, and other sexual crimes

- New material to measure victimization by nonstrangers, including domestic violence

Anatomy of a Crime

Although the crime rate has been declining since the early 1990s, public opinion polls indicate that citizens' fear of crime remains high. Individuals live in fear of being victimized by certain types of crime, and this fear may not have a foundation in fact. Many people, for example, may keep guns in their homes as protection against the nighttime intruder, although burglars rarely enter a home if it is likely to be occupied. Myths abound for many types of crime, and unrealistic fear creates a false sense of insecurity and may negatively impact the quality of life for many people.

To demonstrate the difference between perception and reality, an examination of a specific crime may be appropriate. If a crime is dissected and the statistics associated with it are analyzed, public safety and security personnel may be in a better position to educate the public to overcome fear. The examination here involves the anatomy of a burglary.

The old common law definition of a burglary included the breaking and entering of a dwelling house in the nighttime with the intent to commit a felony therein. Under modern statutes, the definition has been simplified and expanded to include virtually any building and, in some cases, motor vehicles. Today, burglary may be defined generally as the entering of a structure to commit a felony or steal property of any value.

Contrary to common belief, the rate of household burglaries has been declining since the early 1970s. In addition, as household income rises, the burglary rate tends to drop. Burglars tend to operate within a community with which they are familiar because knowing the community helps the burglar with identification of access and escape routes. Because burglary often is motivated by economic gain, the burglar, already impoverished, preys on poor homeowners and tenants. A burglar also evaluates potential targets on the basis of the contents and any security measures on the premises. Two thirds of all residential burglaries occur when no one is home. In addition, people tend to become creatures of habit, and it is not difficult for a burglar to identify the routine of a residential target. The proportion of daytime burglaries has increased, primarily because more women have entered the workforce, and the residence is unoccupied during regular daytime business hours. As one can see, the fear of being assaulted in one's own home by a burglar is misplaced.

CAUSES OF CRIME

The scientific study of the causes of crime or behavior that resembles criminal behavior is referred to as *criminology*. In its broadest context, criminology may be defined as the study of violation of norms or antisocial behavior. In its narrowest sense, criminology could be defined as the study of deviant behavior as it relates to violations of the criminal law.

The exact causes of crime are not actually known. However, there are many different views or theories as to what causes crime. Students of human behavior traditionally have been interested in crime and delinquency and have developed theories even though many variables that contribute to the causes of crime cannot be isolated. Many theories, for example, do not account for what social scientists refer to as the negative case, that is, the individual or group of individuals who, even though exposed to the theoretical cause, do not become criminal. Although the causes of crime may not be explainable in specific terms, or through single theories, a variety of theories about the causes of crime have developed. A summary of these theoretical causes follows.

Psychological Theories

Psychological theories relative to crime causation fall into two basic categories. They are *ego-state theories* and *personality-disorder theories*.

Sigmund Freud, the father of ego-state theories, believed that the personality was divided into three parts: (1) the id, which is the source of all basic drives such as hunger and sex; (2) the ego, which is developed during infancy and early childhood and provides the id with a conscious avenue to acquire satisfaction of the drives; and (3) the superego, which is the conscience and inhibits immediate satisfaction of the id. According to the theory, criminal behavior results from a conflict between the id and the superego. In other words, crime occurs because the satisfaction of the basic drives may be inhibited by limited avenues for success. When the desires of the id are in conflict with societal demands, impulses of the id are repressed. If the individual is unable to repress these impulses, criminal behavior may result.

The second group of psychological theories includes theories on personality disorders. These would include theories related to mental deficiency, which is subnormal rather than abnormal behavior. The second type of personality disorder would be psychopathy or sociopathy. A person with such a disorder has a repressed conscience, or superego, is hostile and aggressive on occasion, and usually wants immediate satisfaction of desires. The third type of personality disorder is psychosis. A person with psychosis has lost touch with reality. The criminally insane are examples of persons with psychotic personalities.

Sociological Theories

Sociological theories relative to crime causation focus on the impact of external forces on the individual. These include ecological, cultural, and social influences. Ecological influences include the environment in which one lives or works.

Cultural influences include subcultural norms of, for example, an age group or gang that contribute to crime and delinquency. Notable among cultural theories is Edwin Sutherland's theory of differential association, which proposes that excessive exposure to a certain set of values is conducive to the behaviors espoused by the values. Finally, social influences that could contribute to delinquent or criminal behavior include an abnormal family life as well as problems in school, work, or a recreational setting.

Physiological Theories

Physiological theories include theories that deal with heredity, biochemicals in the human body, and anthropology. Heredity theories propose that crime is passed from one generation to the next. Heredity theories tend to disregard the role of external forces in contributing to delinquent behavior. Biochemical theories focus on hormonal imbalances in the human body and the influences of the secretions of the endocrine glands. Anthropological theories, first developed by Cesare Lombroso in nineteenth century Italy, correlate specific physical features with criminal behavior. In other words, unattractiveness may influence social experiences, which in turn contribute to antisocial behavior.

Other Theoretical Causes

Beyond psychological, sociological, and physiological theories, several other theoretical "causes" of crime have developed. These include the following:

- Economic theories, which focus on the role of unemployment and poverty (Note: The crime rate declined during the Great Depression.)
- Drug culture theories, which focus on the enforcement of drug laws that push up drug prices; users may commit secondary crimes (such as burglary or robbery) to support a drug habit
- Demographic theories, which focus on the changing composition of the population (Young people tend to commit most street crime.)
- Urbanization theories, which focus on a society that is changing from primarily rural to primarily urban; therefore more people are concentrated in smaller areas
- Cultural difference theories, which focus on cultural conflict within a society (Single-culture, homogeneous societies tend to have low crime rates.)
- Expectation level theories, which focus on the disparity between the rich and the poor (As the gap widens between the poor and the affluent, and the ability to become affluent diminishes, frustration among the poor grows and may result in crime.)

- Changing moral standards theories, which focus on changes in "acceptable behavior." (What is acceptable today may be in conflict with outmoded laws related to sexual behavior, pornography, and political correctness.)
- Statistical efficiency theories, which focus on crime rates. It is possible that the number of crimes per capita has not increased since record keeping was begun. It could be that more crime is reported and, therefore, more crime appears in the official statistics.

In the final analysis, most crime may be the result of a multicausal situation. Therefore it may be difficult to isolate single causes in an individual case and treat the cause. This is very problematic for the criminal justice system because effectively dealing with the causes of crime may be beyond the control of public safety agencies.

CRIME PREVENTION STRATEGIES

Crime prevention begins in the high chair and not the electric chair. This statement is not far from the truth when one considers that one's value system is fairly well internalized by the time one reaches school age. Simply stated, how one is treated during the formative and developmental years (1 through 5 years of age) by a parent, guardian, or other family members determines, to a great extent, personality development and acceptable behavior.

Crime prevention strategies include education, treatment, diversion, rehabilitation, and deterrence through law enforcement and security. These strategies, to be effective, involve a collaborative effort between and among individuals, groups, and institutions. It is extremely unlikely that a single cause contributes to delinquent or criminal behavior. Therefore it is necessary for individuals, families, human service agencies, schools, and public safety organizations to work together to prevent or reduce the likelihood of criminal behavior. To date, the criminal justice system has experienced little notable success in preventing the recurrence of criminal behavior by those who have been exposed to the "system." Positive intervention or at the very least deterrence before a crime is committed may be the ultimate solution.

REFERENCES

Albanese, J.S. 1996. *Organized crime in America.* Cincinnati: Anderson.

Brown, S. E., F. A. Esbensen, and G. Geis. 1996. *Criminology: Exploring crime and its context.* 2d ed. Cincinnati: Anderson.

Bureau of Justice Statistics. 1992. *Criminal victimization in the United States, 1991.* Washington, D.C.: U.S. Department of Justice.

Coleman, J. W. 1994. *The criminal elite: The sociology of white collar crime.* New York: St. Martin's Press.

Hakim, S., and E. A. Blackstone. 1997. *Securing home and business: A guide to the electronic security industry.* Woburn, Mass.: Butterworth-Heinemann.

Schmalleger, F. 1997. *Criminal justice: A brief introduction.* 2d ed. Upper Saddle River, N.J.: Prentice-Hall.

Sutherland, E. 1949. *White collar crime.* New York: Dryden.

United States Department of Justice. 1988. *Uniform crime reporting: National incident-based reporting system.* Vol. 1. *Data Collection Guidelines.* Washington, D.C.: U.S. Government Printing Office.

United States Department of Justice, Federal Bureau of Investigation. 1997. *Uniform crime report.* Washington, D.C.: U.S. Government Printing Office.

United States Department of Justice, Office of Justice Programs, Bureau of Justice Statistics. 1997. *Criminal victimization in the United States 1994.* Washington, D.C.: National Criminal Justice Reference Service.

Walker, S. 1983. *The police in America: An introduction.* New York: McGraw-Hill.

Chapter 2

Safety and Security Concerns: Noncriminal

In addition to the threat from criminal activity, there are many other safety and security concerns. Loss prevention and asset protection strategies in the public safety and security arena must focus on potential harm resulting from chemical abuse, fire, environmental misfortune, natural disasters, civil disturbances, and civil liability.

CHEMICAL ABUSE

Nature and Extent

The abuse of alcohol and drugs has become increasingly costly, both economically and in human terms. According to a study released in August of 1996 by the U.S. Department of Health and Human Services, drug use among 12 to 17 year olds more than doubled between 1992 and 1995. In addition, drug abuse in the workplace has become more common. This creates serious problems for society, the employer, and the individual.

Commonly Abused Chemicals

The commonly abused chemicals and the way they are typically ingested include:

- Alcohol, swallowed
- Hallucinogens, swallowed
- PCP, smoked
- Amphetamine (stimulant), swallowed
- Heroin, injected
- Cocaine hydrochloride, snorted or injected
- Cocaine base, smoked
- Methamphetamine, snorted or injected

- Depressants and tranquilizers, swallowed
- Cannabis (marijuana), smoked

Symptoms of Chemical Abuse

The behavioral symptoms of chemical abuse include the following:

- Significant change in personal appearance for the worse
- Sudden and irrational flare-ups
- Unusual degrees of activity or inactivity
- Sudden and dramatic changes in discipline and job performance
- Dilated pupils or wearing sunglasses at inappropriate times or places
- Needle marks or razor cuts, or long sleeves constantly worn to hide such marks
- Sudden attempts to borrow money or to steal
- Frequent association with known drug abusers or pushers

A person exhibiting the symptoms of hallucinogen use (i.e., LSD, peyote, psilo-cybin) may have dilated pupils, sweat excessively, hallucinate, and have increased respiratory and heart rates. The symptoms associated with PCP use may include high pain tolerance, great physical strength, hallucinations, unpredictability, aggressive and extremely violent behavior, excessive sweating, drowsiness, nys-tagmus, paranoia, confusion, blank stares, muscle rigidity, unusual gait, convul-sions, and a possible chemical odor on the breath or body. Symptoms of stimulant use (i.e., cocaine, amphetamines, or methamphetamine) include restlessness, talkativeness, trembling, dilated pupils, sleeplessness, hyperactivity, and in-creased respiratory and heart rates. Finally, symptoms of depressant use (i.e., barbiturates, sedatives, tranquilizers) include slurred speech, poor coordination, unsteadiness, intoxicated behavior with no odor of alcoholic beverages, nystag-mus, and decreased respiratory and heart rate.

Prevention and Treatment Strategies

Primary prevention and treatment strategies have included programs such as Drug Abuse Resistance Education (DARE) and law enforcement emphasis on drug law enforcement and interdiction (the war on drugs). To date, studies have indicated that the DARE program and the war on drugs have had little appreciable impact on reducing illicit drug use. It is interesting to note that a Rand Corporation report published in 1995 indicated that the impact of each dollar spent in drug treatment is approximately the same as seven dollars spent for the war on drugs. Private strategies have included prevention and treatment programs sponsored by health care organizations, private rehabilitation facilities, and employer-sponsored employee assistance programs. Appropriate employer responses to chemical abuse necessarily involve a written and communicated policy, documentation of incidents of abuse in the workplace, and employer intervention through counseling, treatment, probation, and termination. It should be noted that private employers currently have no legal right to intervene unless the chemical abuse affects job performance and safety.

Drug Testing

Drug testing in the workplace is increasing, although the legality of such testing has yet to be firmly established. Current statutes and case law should be consulted to obtain up-to-date information regarding the legality of drug testing in public as well as private practice.

FIRE

Few events can cause as much personal injury or property damage as a fire. Approaches to fire safety include strategies for fire prevention as well as protection. The former applies to policies and procedures that focus on preventing a fire from occurring. The latter involves minimizing personal injury and damage to property once a fire has started.

The nature of fire may be explained simply by addressing the three major components of the classic fire triangle: heat, fuel, and oxygen. All three must be present in appropriate amounts and under appropriate conditions for a fire to occur. Products of combustion include flame, heat, smoke, and invisible toxic gases. From a life-safety standpoint, limiting exposure to all products of combustion is extremely critical. Exposure to flame and heat may cause serious injury and death within a very short time. Smoke obscures vision and exit routes. Toxic gases displace life-sustaining oxygen. Most fire deaths result from the inhalation of toxic gases.

Classifications of fire include the following:

- Class A—ordinary combustibles such as paper and wood
- Class B—flammable liquids such as gasoline
- Class C—electrical
- Class D—combustible metals

Fire prevention involves controlling the fire triangle. It involves strategies and tactics designed to prevent a fire from occurring in the first place. It also involves training and education of individuals as well as organizations about the nature, extent, and realities of fire and its prevention.

Once a fire has started, protection strategies are used to minimize the damage and spread of fire. These strategies typically include the use of personnel and fire protection and suppression equipment such as alarms, extinguishers, sprinkler systems, and fire-fighting equipment. Strategies also include the use of fire escapes, exits, evacuation procedures, and fire doors to help contain the fire.

ENVIRONMENTAL MISFORTUNE

Environmental misfortune includes accidents, medical emergencies, exposure to hazardous materials, power failures, and gas line or water main breaks. In addition to the possibility of personal injury or death, direct costs associated with these events include increases in medical insurance premiums and worker compensation claims. Indirect costs include lost productivity. To assist in the creation of a safer working environment, Congress passed the Occupational Safety and Health Act (OSHA) in 1970. This law outlines specific requirements for employers. According to the law, employers must do the following:

- Know and comply with OSHA regulations and standards
- Eliminate hazards and provide a safe and healthy work environment
- Establish a record-keeping and reporting system that covers all work-related injuries, deaths, and illnesses
- Conduct periodic safety and health inspections and correct any hazards found
- Allow the Occupational Safety and Health Administration to inspect their facilities
- Provide protective equipment
- Keep workers informed about their rights, the company's safety record, and safety standards
- Develop and enforce safety and health standards
- Provide safety training for employees

Most accidents result from carelessness, failure to have or follow safety rules, and horseplay. Medical emergencies can occur at any time, and employees should be trained to respond properly. Hazardous materials emergencies require extreme care because of the volatile nature of toxic gases, chemicals, liquids, and corrosive materials. Utility failures also may be life threatening, and back-up systems and procedures should be planned.

NATURAL DISASTERS

A natural disaster may be defined as any sudden, extraordinary misfortune in nature. Types of natural disasters include earthquakes, tornadoes, hurricanes, forest fires, floods, and storms. Any natural disaster can result in injuries, deaths, and property loss. Floods, for example, contribute to a greater loss of life in the United States than any other type of natural disaster. Contingency plans should be developed in advance of any natural disaster. These plans should involve an assessment of the potential risk, prioritization of tasks necessary to prevent or reduce losses, preparation for various disaster scenarios, and a plan to recover from the disaster.

CIVIL DISTURBANCES

A civil disturbance, or disorder, may be defined as any group activity that disrupts the normal peace and tranquility of a neighborhood or community. These activities can be legal or illegal. Examples include strikes and labor disputes, demonstrations, special events (sporting, concerts, parades), and riots. Any nonviolent group can become violent if conditions conducive to violence exist. The potential for property loss, injuries, and death is tremendous. The riot in Los Angeles that began on April 29, 1992, subsequent to the acquittal of police officers involved in the Rodney King incident, resulted in more than $1 billion in losses, 10,000 businesses destroyed, at least 1,300 injuries, and 44 deaths. The damage and casualties were greater than those of the Los Angeles (Watts) riot in 1965 and the Detroit riots of 1967. As with natural disasters, contingency plans should be developed to deal with civil disturbances and minimize property loss and casualties.

CIVIL LIABILITY

In the latter part of the twentieth century, liability became a major concern for public as well as private organizations and institutions. Courts increasingly have been awarding huge settlements to plaintiffs who file and prove claims of sexual harassment, unsafe or insecure environments, negligence, invasion of privacy, excessive use of force, and violations of civil rights. The incidents that precipitate these claims involve intentional or unintentional wrongs, failure to protect, and failure to exercise a reasonable standard of care.

In some cases, liability may be imposed even though an individual is not at fault or did not intend any wrong (strict liability). In other cases, employers, other organizations, or third parties may be held liable for the actions of their employees or other person with whom they have a relationship (vicarious liability). One way to reduce liability is to hire the right people and maintain their integrity. A comprehensive plan for reducing liability includes a human resource management strategy that contains policies and procedures, training, supervision, discipline, provision for review and revision of policies and procedures, and legal support.

REFERENCES

Gallagher, G. P. 1990. The six-layered liability protection system for police. *The Police Chief* 57 (June): 40–44.

Hess, K. M., and H. M. Wrobleski. 1996. *Introduction to private security.* 4th ed. Minneapolis: West.

Papi, V. 1994. Planning before disaster strikes. *Security Concepts* 2 (February): 6, 19.

Chapter 3

Legal Aspects of Safety and Security

The importance of knowing law cannot be overemphasized. A working knowledge of, and appreciation for, the law assists any individual, business, or agency with the protection of personnel, property, clients or consumers, and the company or agency itself. Knowing the law and following legal guidelines helps everyone avoid liability and work within the limits of authority or scope of practice.

Law may be defined generally as rules of conduct that pertain to a given political order of society. These rules of conduct are backed by the organized force of the community.

The sources of law include the United States Constitution, federal statutes, state constitutions and statutes, ordinances, administrative regulations, judicial decisions (case law), and common law (law based on custom or tradition). Common law originated in England and formed the foundation for U.S. law. Today, however, many jurisdictions, including California, no longer recognize any form of common law.

Types of law include those that relate to the public and those that relate to private individuals and businesses. Public law includes criminal law (both substantive and procedural), evidence, constitutional law, and regulations promulgated by administrative agencies. Private law refers to contracts, torts (a civil wrong for which the law provides a remedy), and property law.

CRIMINAL LAW

Overview

A crime may be defined simply as an offense against society. In other words, when a criminal offense has been committed, the offender has committed an offense against the society that has designated that behavior criminal. Therefore, if a person violates a state criminal law, the offense is committed against the citizens of that state regardless of who the specific victim is. Likewise, when one commits a violation of the federal criminal code, the offense is committed against all of the citizens of the United States.

A more comprehensive definition of crime is that it is an intentional act or omission to act in violation of the criminal law (penal code) committed without defense or justification and sanctioned (punished) by society (government) as a felony or misdemeanor. The essential elements of the crime include criminal intent (a design, resolve, or purpose of the mind), an act, or, in some cases, omission to act, and a causal connection between the intent and the act itself. The corpus delicti of a crime includes injury, loss or harm, *and* the existence of a human criminal agent as its cause.

Types of intent fall into four categories: general, specific, transferred, and criminal negligence. General criminal intent may be inferred from merely doing the act. Specific criminal intent requires a specifically intended and desired result. With transferred, or constructive, intent, a person may be liable for unintended consequences. For example, in the latter situation, if A shoots B with intent to kill, but misses and kills C, an unintended victim, the intent to kill is "transferred" to C. Criminal negligence is the failure to exercise the degree of care a reasonable and prudent person would exercise under the same circumstances.

In addition, one must be not only the actual cause of the events leading to the result but also the proximate or legal cause whereby the actor should have foreseen the result. One is liable if the result is foreseeable. Normally, one is responsible for one's own actions. In some cases, such as employer-employee relationships, the employer may be vicariously liable for the actions of the employee.

Crimes are classified generally as felonies, misdemeanors, and infractions. Felonies usually carry a potential penalty of 1 year or more in prison. Misdemeanors carry a potential penalty of up to 1 year in county jail. Infractions typically carry a potential penalty of a fine and are not usually punishable by imprisonment.

The remaining pages in this section present a brief summary of parties to a crime, defenses, and basic definitions of several crimes commonly encountered by public safety and security personnel. Also presented is an overview of the laws of arrest and policy regarding use of force. The reader is advised to refer to individual state statutory provisions for more detailed information regarding local crimes and elements.

Parties to a Crime

At common law, there were four possible parties to a crime. The principal in the first degree was the person who actually was present and consummated the crime. The principal in the second degree was the person who was constructively present at the crime scene. For example, the driver in a getaway car waiting outside during a store robbery would be "constructively" present in the store. The accessory before the fact was an individual who was neither actually nor constructively present during the crime but who aided (provided assistance) or abetted (encouraged) the commission of the crime before it was committed. The accessory after the fact was the person who was unaware that a crime was committed until after the event and then aided or abetted the principals or accessories before the fact.

Under modern statutes the principals in the first and second degree as well as the accessory before the fact are treated as principals. However, these statutes generally retain the classification of accessory after the fact for a felony because being unaware of the crime until after it was committed, there is nothing that the accessory after the fact could have done to prevent it.

Defenses to (Justification for) Crime

A defendant in a criminal case may be able to establish a legitimate justification or excuse for what might otherwise be classified as criminal behavior. A partial list of these defenses and their definitions follow.

1. Capacity to commit crime.
   - Infancy—those under the age of 14, absent clear proof to the contrary, are generally not held criminally liable for their actions
   - Diminished capacity—those with an intelligence quotient of 24 or less (idiots), those in an unconscious state, those who are intoxicated involuntarily, or those who are intoxicated voluntarily where the crime requires specific criminal intent
   - Physical impossibility—those who are physically incapable of the crime
   - Insanity—those who, because of a mental disease or defect, are unable to understand the difference between right and wrong
2. Mistake of fact. Except for the most serious offenses, ignorance or mistake of fact may be a defense.
3. Mistake of law. Mistake of law generally is not a defense unless confusion exists as to the law violated. For example, the finder of lost property may advertise it in the lost and found column of a local newspaper when local law requires that the property be turned over to the local police.
4. Duress. Except for the most serious crimes, i.e., those punishable by death or imprisonment for life, duress may be a defense if the offense was committed when, because of a threat, the actor reasonably believed human life was in immediate danger.
5. Entrapment. Law enforcement officers or someone working in conjunction with law enforcement entice another to commit a crime the person was not otherwise predisposed to commit. Merely providing the opportunity to commit a crime, e.g., an undercover officer making a drug buy from a known dealer, is not entrapment.
6. Self-defense. One reasonably believes one's life or the life of an innocent third person is in danger of serious bodily injury or death.
7. Necessity. Out of necessity, the actor behaves in a way that would normally create criminal liability except the circumstances dictate the behavior. An

example of this situation would be when an accident victim breaks into a home in a remote area to use the telephone to call for emergency assistance. The individual may still be monetarily liable for any damages caused.

Preliminary (Preparatory) Offenses

- Criminal attempt—an attempt to commit some other crime coupled with a direct but ineffectual act completed toward the commission of the intended crime
- Solicitation—soliciting another to commit an intended crime
- Conspiracy—two or more persons who agree to commit any crime coupled with an overt act in furtherance of the conspiracy

Obstruction of Justice (Inchoate Offenses)

- Perjury—willfully lying under oath or affirmation
- Subordination of perjury—procuring someone else to commit perjury
- Bribery—asking, giving, accepting, or offering anything of value to another with specific intent to corruptly influence any act, decision, vote, opinion, or other official function or duty of such person

Offenses against the Public Peace

- Disturbing the peace—unlawfully fighting in a public place or challenging another person in a public place to fight, maliciously and willfully disturbing another person by loud and unreasonable noise, or using offensive words in a public place that are inherently likely to produce an immediate violent reaction
- Unlawful assembly—two or more persons assembled with the intent to do an unlawful act or a lawful act in a violent manner
- Riot—two or more persons acting together without authority of law to use any force or violence in a manner calculated to inspire terror

Offenses against Property

- Theft (larceny)—intentionally taking and carrying away the personal property of another with the intent to permanently deprive the owner thereof
- Fictitious check—willfully, with intent to defraud, writing or delivering a check, knowing at the time there are insufficient funds for payment in full
- False pretenses—knowingly, by false pretense or fraud, procuring money, labor, or property of another

- Embezzlement—fraudulent appropriation of property by a person to whom it has been entrusted
- Breaking and entering—forcibly entering a structure intended for human occupancy without the permission of the owner or lessee and destroying property of value in or around the structure
- Burglary—entry of a structure with the intent to commit a felony or steal property of any value (Note: Some states also have a "breaking" requirement.)
- Arson—wilfully and maliciously setting fire to or causing to be burned, any structure, forest land, or property
- Forgery—the false making or material alteration of any document that, if genuine, would be of apparent legal efficacy (carry with it a legal obligation or responsibility)
- Extortion (blackmail)—obtaining property from another with the victim's consent through the threat of some future harm

Offenses against Persons

- Assault—an attempted battery or placing someone in fear of an immediate battery
- Battery—wilfully and unlawfully using force or violence on another person; any harmful, offensive, and unconsented-to contact with the victim is sufficient to constitute battery
- Robbery—the felonious taking of property from another in the victim's presence against the victim's will by the wrongful use of force or fear
- False imprisonment—unlawfully restricting the personal liberty of another
- Kidnapping—generally, the forcible abduction of a person to another location
- Rape—generally, any unconsented-to sexual intercourse upon the person of another
- Unlawful sexual intercourse (statutory rape)—the act of sexual intercourse with a person under the age of 18 who is not the spouse of the perpetrator
- Homicide (unlawful—justifiable and excusable homicides are not unlawful)
  1. Murder (first degree)—the willful, deliberate, or premeditated killing of a human being or fetus with malice aforethought or a death that results during the commission of an inherently dangerous felony listed in the first-degree murder statute (the felony murder rule)
  2. Murder (second degree)—the unlawful killing of a human being or fetus with malice aforethought but without premeditation
  3. Manslaughter (voluntary)—the unlawful killing of a human being without malice aforethought but upon a sudden quarrel or in the heat of passion
  4. Manslaughter (involuntary)—the unlawful killing of a human being without malice aforethought in the commission of an unlawful act not amounting to a felony or a lawful act in an unlawful or negligent manner (example: vehicular homicide)

Controlled Substances Laws

Controlled substances laws cover acts such as the possession, sale, transportation, manufacture, furnishing, and administering of controlled substances listed in applicable state and federal statutes. These laws also refer to the possession of drug paraphernalia and being under the influence of, or cultivating, a controlled substance. These laws focus generally on narcotics, cocaine, heroin, controlled substances, amphetamines, barbiturates, and marijuana.

Public Safety and Morals Offenses

Public safety and morals offenses generally refer to offenses associated with pornography, obscene matter, sexual exploitation of minors, contributing to the delinquency of minors, incest, indecent exposure, loitering, and prostitution.

Laws of Arrest

A law enforcement officer generally may make an arrest in the case of a felony committed in the officer's presence. The officer may also arrest for a felony not committed in the officer's presence if there is probable cause to believe that a felony was committed and that the arrestee committed it. If no felony crime was committed, a police officer is protected from civil and criminal liability. For misdemeanors, a law enforcement officer may arrest for a misdemeanor committed in the officer's presence. If the misdemeanor is not committed in the officer's presence, an arrest cannot be made unless an arrest warrant is on file for the arrestee.

A private security person (or citizen not a police officer) generally may make an arrest in the case of a felony committed in the person's presence. In the case of a felony not committed in the person's presence, an arrest can be made if the felony was, *in fact*, committed and the arresting person has probable cause to believe that the person arrested committed it. A security officer or private citizen also may arrest for a misdemeanor committed in the arresting person's presence. However, security officers or private persons have no authority to arrest for a misdemeanor not committed in their presence. Furthermore, a private security officer or citizen is not protected from criminal or civil liability due to false imprisonment or false arrest.

Use of Force

As a general rule, persons can use whatever force is reasonably necessary, including deadly force, to protect themselves or an innocent third party from serious bodily harm or death. A person may use nondeadly force in the protection of property.

EVIDENCE

Overview

Evidence consists of testimony, writings, material objects, and other things presented to the senses to prove the existence or nonexistence of a fact. The rules of evidence govern the admissibility of testimony, writings, and material objects in judicial proceedings. Proof is the establishment by evidence of a requisite degree of belief concerning a fact in the mind of the trier of fact (jury) or the court (judge). It is the desired result of evidence. Burden of proof is the obligation to produce evidence sufficient to prove a fact or set of facts.

Evidence is offered in court as an item of proof to impeach (or discredit) a witness, to rehabilitate (or support) a witness, and to assist in determining a sentence (e.g., aggravating circumstances in determinate sentences, proving "no probation" offense elements, special circumstances in death penalty cases). Evidence must be relevant, competently presented, and legally obtained (meets constitutional and statutory safeguards).

Sources of evidence law include the state and federal evidence code provisions regarding witness competency, introduction of writings, privileged communications, and hearsay evidence. Sources also include penal code provisions regarding accomplice testimony, invasion of privacy and wiretapping; the U.S. Constitution and state constitutions; and case law (e.g., search and seizure, Miranda issues, interpretation of evidence code statutes).

Types of Evidence

Types of evidence include the following:

- Testimonial evidence (testimony)—testimony given by a witness, victim, or suspect who has knowledge of the facts being tried in a case
- Documentary evidence (writings)—any documented and tangible form of communication offered as evidence in court, such as notes, journals, ledgers, computer-generated data, photographs, audio tapes, and video tapes
- Real (physical) evidence (material objects)—fruits of the crime, instrumentalities of a crime, and contraband, for example
- Demonstrative evidence—materials such as maps, models, charts, diagrams, displays, and computer simulations meant to portray or enhance the meaning of evidence presented to the trier of fact
- Relevant evidence—evidence that has any tendency to prove or disprove a disputed fact in a case, such as motive for the crime, capacity to commit a crime, opportunity to commit the crime, prior threats or expressions of ill will by the accused, possession of writings or real evidence linking a suspect to the crime, physical evidence linking a suspect to the crime scene, consciousness of

guilt or "admission by conduct" evidence, evidence affecting the credibility of a witness, and modus operandi factors

- Admissions and confessions—an admission is a statement by a suspect acknowledging some fact of relevant evidence in a case. A confession is a statement by a suspect claiming full responsibility for a crime. Both are culpatory and have the tendency to show the guilt of the accused.
- Hearsay evidence—an out-of-court statement presented in court by someone other than the original declarant offered to prove the truth of the matter stated in court
- Consciousness of guilt evidence—conduct by the accused from which an inference of guilt or adoptive admission can be drawn (e.g., running from the crime scene, assaulting an officer, threatening a witness, giving false information, attempts to destroy or conceal evidence, refusal to provide personal physical evidence)

Presentation of Evidence

Evidence is commonly presented in court in the following ways:

- Inferences—a deduction of fact that can be logically and reasonably drawn from a fact or group of facts
- Presumptions—an assumption of fact that the law requires to be made from another fact or group of facts (e.g., presumed innocent until proven guilty)
- Direct evidence—evidence that directly proves a fact without drawing inferences from other facts. For example, if a witness saw the defendant commit a crime, this is argued as direct evidence of the defendant's guilt.
- Circumstantial evidence—evidence that proves a fact through inference or logical association with another fact. For example, if a defendant's latent fingerprints are recovered at a crime scene, it can be inferred the defendant was present even though there is no direct witness to the crime.
- Judicial notice—matters of common fact, general knowledge, or law that are universally known, easily referenced, and not subject to dispute. The evidence can be presented as evidence without adversarial argument. Examples of judicial notice include courses of nature, scientific principles, meanings of words and phrases, geographic and historical facts, legal procedures, and governmental reports.
- Stipulation—an agreement between opposing parties that a fact can be offered into evidence without adversarial argument

Testimonial Evidence

Types of witnesses include the following:

- Lay witness—an ordinary witness, including most police officers, who has some personal knowledge of the facts being tried in a criminal case. As a general rule, a lay witness is permitted to testify only as to what the witness knows as fact (what is actually seen, heard, or otherwise perceived with one's senses) and is not permitted to give an opinion or conclusion in conjunction with testimony. However, there are exceptions. The opinion evidence rule permits a lay witness to give an opinion in court when an event is based on the personal knowledge of the witness and the opinion would be helpful in the clear understanding of the witness's testimony. Common areas qualifying for opinion evidence include state of emotion; appearance and demeanor (intoxication or injuries); speed, distance, measurement, value, and other quantifiable areas; identity and physical characteristics; and physical properties of substances (such as blood and narcotics).
- Expert witness—a witness who possesses some special knowledge, skill, experience, training, or education relevant to the facts being tried in a case. An expert witness is permitted to give an opinion or conclusion in conjunction with testimony. The qualifications of an expert witness are determined by a magistrate during a voir dire ("to speak the truth") examination. Examples of expert testimony in criminal trials include that presented by medical, forensic, psychology, and police experts.

A subpoena is a written order commanding the presence of a witness in court for the purpose of giving testimony. A subpoena duces tecum commands the production of writings or material objects in court. A person can be held in contempt of court for refusing to comply with a subpoena.

Witness Competency and Credibility

A competent witness is properly qualified to give testimony in court. All witnesses, regardless of age, are presumed competent to testify. The burden of proof falls to the side that opposes the witness in court to prove incompetency. The question of competency is decided during a voir dire examination. A witness can be disqualified from testifying if the witness is unable to observe, perceive, recall, narrate, or understand the duty to tell the truth. Common examples of potentially incompetent witnesses include young children, developmentally disabled persons, physically handicapped persons, and foreign language–speaking persons. Credibility is the believability or weight given to a witness's testimony by the trier of fact.

Impeachment attacks the credibility of a witness or lessens the weight of that witness's testimony in the mind of the trier of fact. Impeachment is a hopeful outcome of cross or recross examination. Common impeachment areas include physical or mental state of the witness; bias, interest, or other motive in the case; a witness's general reputation for truthfulness and honesty; a prior felony conviction; or inconsistencies and manner of one's testimony. Rehabilitation of a witness tends to bolster or lend support to credibility of a witness. Rehabilitation is a hopeful outcome of redirect examination.

Documentary Evidence (Writings)

A writing is authenticated when a witness testifies to the method or mode of authorship and preparation. The best evidence is an original writing. Secondary evidence is a copy of the writing offered in lieu of the original writing. In California, a copy is admissible to the same extent as an original writing unless there is a question as to the authenticity of the duplicate or if the admission of the duplicate would be prejudicial.

Photographs of a gruesome, bloody, shocking, or lewd nature are subject to a balancing test by the courts. The judge balances the relevancy of the photographs against their potential prejudicial effect on the defendant. If the judge rules the photographs would so inflame the jury that they would be prejudicial, the photographs are excluded. If the judge rules the probative value (the relative weight of the evidence) of the photographs outweighs prejudice, the photographs are admissible.

Real and Physical Evidence (Material Objects)

Examples of material objects are the following:

- Fruits of the crime—objects acquired as a result of commission of a crime (e.g., stolen property taken in a theft, burglary, or robbery).
- Instrumentalities of a crime—objects used by the perpetrator to commit the crime (e.g., crowbar in a burglary, gun in a murder, knife in an assault with a deadly weapon, scales and packaging materials in a narcotics sales case).
- Contraband—an object prohibited by law and therefore illegal to possess (e.g., narcotics, deadly weapons, child pornography).
- Other physical evidence—the entire range of trace, perishable, and other types of personal identification evidence that have comparable individual identifying characteristics or class characteristics. Examples of physical evidence include fingerprints, blood and biological fluids, ballistics, hairs, fibers, and other trace evidence.

Common rules concerning the introduction of material objects include the following:

- Authentication. A material object is authenticated when a "finder" testifies to the manner or circumstances under which the evidence was recovered.

- Chain of custody. It is necessary to maintain a record of persons who handle the evidence from the point of collection until the time the evidence is presented in court. The purpose is to maintain the integrity of the evidence and counter allegations that the evidence may have been substituted or altered.
- Legal duty to collect and preserve evidence. There is no due process duty on police to collect or preserve real or physical evidence for the defendant. A defendant cannot have a case dismissed on the sole grounds that authorities failed to collect or preserve possible exculpatory evidence at a crime scene. However, a defendant can attempt to impeach the quality or completeness of an investigation by showing that police were negligent and failed to follow proper procedures. The defendant also can attempt to raise a reasonable doubt as to guilt by showing that if the evidence had been collected, it would have pointed to another suspect. As such, the collection and preservation of evidence are always a professional obligation and at times essential to the prosecution in proving criminal guilt.

Privileges and Privileged Communications

A privilege is a constitutional or statutory provision that a witness can legally use to refuse to testify in court. Even though a witness may possess personal knowledge of the facts being tried in the case, if a privilege exists, the witness may refuse to testify and not be found in contempt of court.

Testimonial Privileges

Testimonial privileges include the following:

- Privilege against self-incrimination. As a rule, a criminal defendant cannot be compelled to take the witness stand and testify and can legally refuse to disclose information that may tend to self-incriminate. However, if a defendant takes the witness stand and testifies, the privilege is waived, and the defendant can be cross-examined about any matter brought out during direct examination. This privilege does not apply to the collection of personal identification and physical evidence during a criminal investigation, because this evidence is nontestimonial (nonverbal) in nature.
- Husband-wife testimonial privilege. As a rule, one spouse can refuse to be a witness against the other spouse during the course of a legal marriage. The testimonial privilege applies to observations, conversations, and findings. Only the witness-spouse can claim this privilege; the other spouse has no blocking power. The testimonial privilege is void when a crime is committed against the spouse, family members, or other member of the household. If the marriage

ends through divorce or annulment, the testimonial privilege ends, and the former spouse must then testify if subpoenaed.

- Officer-informant privilege. A peace officer has the testimonial privilege to refuse to disclose the identify of an informant who provided official information during the course and scope of the officer's duties. However, if this informant is a material witness on the issue of innocence or guilt of the accused, the defense is entitled to the informant's name and address. If an officer still claims privilege, the officer cannot be held in contempt of court, but the defendant is entitled to case dismissal on due-process grounds. The potential materiality of an informant is determined by the judge during an in camera (in chambers) hearing.
- News shield privilege. A news reporter has the testimonial privilege to refuse to disclose the source of news information. This privilege does not apply to the actual witnessing of a criminal event. A news reporter or news organization has the privilege to refuse to disclose any unpublished information not released to the general public through electronic or print media. This privilege does not apply to published information.

Confidential Communications Privileges

Confidential communications privileges include the following:

- Husband-wife confidential communications privilege. One spouse may refuse to disclose, and the other spouse can block the disclosure of, a confidential communication made during the course of a legal marriage. Both spouses may claim this privilege as long as the oral or written communication was made for spouse's "ears or eyes" only. The confidential communication privilege is void when a crime is committed against the spouse, family members, or other member of the household, or if the disclosure is made to another or in the known presence of a third party. The confidential communication privilege survives termination of the marriage.
- Attorney-client privilege. An attorney can refuse to disclose, or a client can block the disclosure of, a confidential communication made during the course of an attorney-client relationship. This privilege is meant to allow a free exchange between attorney and client without fear these conversations will be disclosed later in court. This privilege does not apply to planning the commission of a crime in the future.
- Clergy-penitent privilege. A clergy person can refuse to disclose, or a penitent can block the disclosure of, a confidential penitential communication made for the purposes of spiritual advice and absolution.
- Physician-patient privilege. A physician can refuse to disclose, or a patient can block the disclosure of, a confidential communication made for the purpose of medical diagnosis and treatment. However, the physician-patient privilege

does not apply to criminal court testimony. Conversations about crime-related events void the privilege, and a physician must testify in court.

Hearsay Evidence

Hearsay evidence is a statement made by someone other than the witness who is testifying in court and offered by the witness to prove the truth of a matter stated. Most often, hearsay arises when a witness attempts to testify about what someone else said outside court. As a rule, hearsay evidence is inadmissible unless the testimony falls under a recognized hearsay exception. Exceptions to the hearsay rule include the following:

- Admissions and confessions. Inculpatory statements by the accused are admissible when repeated by a peace officer or private person as long as the statement was legally obtained. A statement that is adverse to one's own interest is presumed truthful enough to be repeated by another.
- Dying declaration. A statement by a dying person that relates to the cause and circumstances surrounding the person's death is admissible hearsay. The victim must be under an impending sense of death (i.e., lost hope of recovery); the statement must concern the victim's personal knowledge about the cause of death; and the victim must subsequently die. The law presumes a person nearing death would have no reason to lie and would want to die with a clear conscience. Thus a person would have no reason to be untruthful. If a victim survives, the statement may still be admissible under the spontaneous statement or prior statement of witnesses exceptions to hearsay.
- Spontaneous statements. A statement made under stress, close in time to a crime, and about what the declarant saw or otherwise perceived is admissible hearsay. A spontaneous statement can be offered by a peace officer or private person receiving or overhearing the statement. Statements made under the heat of excitement are considered trustworthy because the declarant has no time to premeditate or deliberate a falsehood. Thus the statement reflects the declarant's true perceptions of the event. If there has been a substantial time lapse between the crime and the utterance based on the totality of circumstances, the reliability of this statement can be questioned.
- Business and official records. Records and other writings kept in the normal course of business or government operation are presumed trustworthy. These records can be authenticated and interpreted by any person in the organization familiar with their preparation and content. It is not absolutely necessary to have the original preparer of the writing testify in court. The records must be prepared in a standardized manner by a person who has personal knowledge of the event recorded, and the information must be recorded close in time to the incident or transaction recorded.
- Prior statements of witnesses, past recollection recorded. Once a witness testifies under oath and is subject to examination, a prior statement made by that

witness is admissible for the purposes of impeaching an inconsistent statement or rehabilitating an incomplete statement. Notes or recorded statements of the witness can be admitted for the same purposes.

- Hearsay testimony at preliminary hearings. Law enforcement officers with more than 5 years experience or who have completed a related training course are allowed to give hearsay evidence at preliminary hearings for the purpose of determining whether the defendant has committed a felony crime. The officer must have talked personally to a victim, witness, investigator, or expert witness to offer this hearsay testimony. "Totem pole" (multiple level) hearsay or merely reading into the court record a report by an uninvolved officer is not permitted under this rule.

Search and Seizure

The law with respect to search and seizure is very detailed. The following discussion includes definitions of the various terms associated with search and seizure as well as an explanation of proper procedures for conducting legal searches.

Reasonable searches are permitted under the Fourth Amendment and one does not always need a search warrant to conduct a lawful search and seizure. A *search* involves intrusion into an area where a person has a reasonable expectation of privacy. The purpose of a search is to find evidence or contraband to be used in a criminal prosecution. A *seizure* occurs when a person's freedom of movement is restricted or when property is taken into custody. A seizure involves meaningful interference with a person's movement or property interest.

Probable cause involves facts that would lead a person of ordinary care and prudence to believe and conscientiously entertain a strong and honest suspicion that evidence or contraband will be found in or at a particular location. An officer may seek a search warrant or conduct a warrantless vehicle search on the basis of probable cause. The scope of a probable cause search is limited by the scope and circumstances under which it is being conducted. The scope of a lawful search also is regulated by the circumstances under which the search is being conducted. The two elements for determining the legal scope of a search are, first, what the officer is looking for (i.e., evidence, contraband, weapons, victims, or suspects), and, second, where the officer is likely to find it (i.e., is it reasonable for the officer to find the object or person in the area being searched). Evidence or contraband recovered outside the lawful scope of a search can be subject to suppression.

The *exclusionary rule* requires that any evidence obtained by the government or its agents in violation of U.S. constitutional rights be excluded at trial. The main purposes of the exclusionary rule are ① to deter misconduct by peace officers by eliminating the incentive for unconstitutional behavior and prohibiting the admission of evidence obtained illegally and ② to maintain the integrity of the judiciary by keeping tainted evidence out of the courtroom. Illegally seized evidence is inadmissible in court, and any evidence that directly stems from this evidence also is inadmissible.

The *plain view doctrine* holds that anything in plain view is not constitutionally protected. There are two elements to the plain view doctrine. First, the officer must have probable cause to believe the object or property observed constitutes evidence of a crime. Second, the officer must have a legal position or the "right to be" where the observation is made. A plain view observation can serve as the basis for seizure of the evidence observed or can prompt another legal basis to search for more evidence or contraband.

A *detention* is a temporary stop for investigation and questioning to determine a person's involvement, if any, in criminal activity. Police officers are able to seize a person's freedom of movement on the basis of reasonable suspicion of criminal activity, short of the reasonable cause needed for a custodial arrest. Detentions must be conducted lawfully, or any evidence or statements subsequently obtained will be inadmissible in court.

No one is permitted to detain at will. For a legal detention to occur, a police officer must have reasonable suspicion that a crime is about to take place, is taking place, or has taken place and that the person to be detained is connected with suspected criminal activity. Reasonable suspicion is factually based on detention factors such as a matching suspect description, matching vehicle description, person in proximity of a recently occurred crime, known high-crime area, person exhibits symptoms of unlawful drug or alcohol consumption, method of criminal operation, flight or furtive movements, and criminal history. Officers may detain a person for a period of time reasonably necessary to accomplish the purpose of the investigation.

A *contact or consensual encounter* is any interaction between a police officer or nonsworn person and citizen that does not involve formal police restraint of that citizen's freedom of movement. A contact does not involve seizure of the person under the Fourth Amendment. During a contact, a person is under no obligation to cooperate with an officer or citizen or answer questions and is free to leave at any time. The following actions are permissible for an officer or citizen during a contact: walking up to a person or a parked vehicle and making inquiries about one's presence in an area; using a flashlight or spotlight for illumination; requesting, examining, and returning identification; and general follow-up conversation on a person's responses to the officer's questions. The following actions would convert a contact into a detention by means of exercising restraint over a person's freedom of movement: using a red light, directing or ordering a person to stop or remain, demanding identification, and retaining identification to conduct a warrants check.

A *frisk* is a cursory pat-down of a legally detained suspect for the purpose of discovering deadly or dangerous weapons that could be used to assault a police officer or other person legally authorized to arrest. A frisk can be lawfully conducted when a person has been detained for a crime involving weapons; for instrumentalities that could be used as weapons; or for an offense that threatens violent conduct. A frisk also may be conducted during a contact or nonviolent detention with consent of the suspect. The scope of a frisk is for hard objects that could be reasonably articulated as weapons. Hard objects can be retrieved, examined, and retained during the detention for officer safety. If the object is an instrumentality or contraband, reasonable cause for a police officer to arrest exists. Soft bulges must be retrieved under another search basis.

A police officer may *incidentally or contemporaneously to a lawful custodial arrest* search the person of the arrestee and the area within the arrestee's immediate control (arm's reach) for any possible evidence, weapons, or contraband. This search would include pockets and containers in the possession of the arrestee. A private person making an arrest may search for weapons only.

When a person is arrested inside a residence or dwelling, a police officer may, incidental to that arrest, search the person of the arrestee and any area within the arrestee's immediate control. This would include cabinets, drawers, furniture, containers, and closets within arm's reach of the arrestee. Some general exceptions permit a police officer to extend beyond the arm's reach limitations after an arrest in a residence or dwelling. These include plain view, protective peek, pathway of suspect, protective sweep, and alternative search basis.

When a person is arrested inside or closely associated with a motor vehicle, a police officer may incidentally to that custodial arrest search all compartments and containers within the passenger area of the vehicle. The passenger area is considered to be within arm's reach of the person arrested. If a police officer has probable cause to believe there is evidence or contraband in a vehicle that is mobile or accessible to the roadway, the police officer may conduct a warrantless search of that vehicle, including compartments and containers. This is referred to as the *automobile exception to the search warrant requirement.* Probable cause involves articulable facts that the objects of the search will be found inside the vehicle. The scope of this search is regulated by the size or nature of the evidence or contraband being sought. If probable cause and the scope of evidence sought are within a closed container, the container may be searched. This includes compartments, the trunk, and locked containers. As part of a police department policy, a police officer may inventory the contents of a lawfully impounded or stored vehicle before towing. This search is based on the general administrative necessity of protecting the officer and agency from allegations of theft or damage, to take an arrestee's valuables or property into custody for safekeeping, and to assure that there are no hazardous objects or materials in the car that could endanger the general public. Evidence found fortuitously in plain view is admissible.

A *search warrant* is an order issued by a judge and directed to a peace officer that commands a search of a described location for described evidence or contraband. The statutory grounds for the issuance of a search warrant must be specified. Search warrants are not required in some search and seizure situations (e.g., mobile vehicles with probable cause and probation or parole searches). Certain search and seizure situations almost always require acquisition of a search warrant (e.g., residential search and body intrusions). Specific rules regarding search warrants include the following:

- A search warrant requires probable cause or facts that would lead a reasonable person to believe there is strong suspicion that evidence or contraband will be found at a particular location. Probable cause can be established through a police officer's personal observations, information received from citizens or other informants, and information received through official channels. Probable cause is communicated to a judge through a written or telephonic affidavit.
- Once issued, a search warrant is good for 10 days and is limited to service between the hours of 7:00 A.M. and 10:00 P.M., unless endorsed upon "good cause" to be served at any time of the day or night. After entry, when the search scene is safe, the police officer should show the original search warrant and provide a copy to a person with a possessory right to the premises.
- Knock and notice rules apply to the service of search warrants. A police officer serving a search warrant must knock, identify and announce purpose, demand entry, and give the person or persons inside a reasonable opportunity to open the door. A factual exigency or emergency circumstance, such as danger to officers, destruction of evidence, or escape of suspect, may excuse knock and notice or permit a contemporaneous entry once an exigency begins. Failure to comply with knock and notice provisions can result in suppression of evidence seized under the authority of the warrant.
- The scope of search is limited to the items and the location listed in the search warrant. Any additional evidence or contraband located in plain view or within the scope of the warrant may be legally seized as fortuitous finds. If additional evidence or contraband observed during the warrant service causes an officer to believe there is more of the same at the premises or location, a second search warrant may be necessary for further legal search for more evidence.
- Officers are required to maintain an inventory of evidence and contraband removed from the search location and file a return with the issuing court.

A *consent search* is one in which a person knowingly and voluntarily waives Fourth Amendment rights after having been given a request-choice. Consent allows a police officer or private person to conduct an exploratory investigation into the area or property where the consenting party has possessory rights. The following rules apply to consent searches:

- Knowingly and voluntarily. *Knowingly* means the person giving the consent waiver has the capacity and mentality to be able to understand the choice to waive or not waive Fourth Amendment rights. *Voluntarily* means the consent to search was given as a result of free will and is not the product of force, coercion, inducement, promise, deceit, trickery, or submission to police authority.
- Request-choice. In asking for consent to search, an officer or private person must request permission to search and such request must be phrased in terms that the decision maker has the choice to refuse the consent.
- Admonition. An officer or private person may choose to advise a person orally

or in writing that the person has the right to refuse to consent to a search to assist in upholding a showing of voluntariness.

- Express or implied waiver. An express waiver is one in which a person agrees to the consent search orally or in writing. An implied waiver is one in which a person agrees to the consent search through affirmative gesture or body language. An equivocal waiver does not constitute legal consent.
- Constitutional considerations. A person has the right to refuse to consent to a search, can limit the area of search, and can stop the search anytime after consent is given. Asserting any of these rights does not constitute consciousness of guilt or probable cause to search further.
- Authority and no authority. The person consenting to a search must be in an authority position. This means the person has possessory rights over the area or property to be searched. Typical no-authority situations include minor children, landlords, visitors, motel managers, babysitters, and household workers. Though these persons may be in charge of a premises or have the right to be in the area, they are not in an authority position to consent to search the area or property.
- Husband-wife rule and exceptions. Generally, one spouse can consent to a search of a jointly occupied house or property, even over the objection of the other spouse. An exception would be "staked out" areas such as dressers, cabinets, storage areas, or other containers of property that are exclusively used by one spouse. Consent must be sought from the spouse who actually uses these areas, or another search basis must be sought.
- Cotenant rule and exceptions. Generally, one cotenant in authority can consent to a search of jointly occupied premises and common areas within, even over the objections of another cotenant. An exception would be "staked out" areas such as a room, dressers, cabinets, storage areas, or other containers of property that are used exclusively by another tenant. Consent must be sought from the other tenant for these areas, or another search basis must be sought.
- Parent-child rule and exceptions. Generally, a parent is in an authority position to consent to police entry into a minor child's room, even if that room is solely occupied by the child. Police would get a plain view inspection of the room. Exceptions still include "staked out" areas or containers of property that the child uses exclusively. Consent must be sought from the child for these areas, or another search basis must be sought. Adult children living with parents fall under the cotenant rule.
- An officer may make a warrantless entry into an area when necessary to protect life, health, or property; to prevent the imminent escape of fleeing suspects; or to prevent the imminent destruction of evidence. These are referred to as *emergency searches*. An exigency involves emergency circumstances requiring swift and immediate action. Any evidence or contraband an officer sees in plain view while searching for victims or suspects is admissible.
- Danger to life or limb. Exigencies include assaults in progress, screams for help, shots fired, domestic violence calls, child endangerment or abuse, 911 calls, medical aid, and suicide attempts.

- Danger of serious property damage. Exigencies include natural disasters, accidents, explosions, clandestine drug labs, fires, burglar alarm soundings, and open doors and windows where there is a possibility of unlawful entry.
- Escape of suspect. A police officer may enter a residence or dwelling in immediate hot pursuit of a suspect running from a crime. If an officer has reasonable cause to arrest a suspect for a felony or misdemeanor that occurred on the street or in a public place, the suspect cannot escape custody by running into a dwelling. Also, under the *investigative pursuit of a serious felon doctrine,* a police officer can make a warrantless entry to search for and arrest a suspect who has committed a dangerous felony involving death or serious bodily injury, even if not in immediate hot pursuit. This entry can be generally made within the first day after the crime or when it is impractical to seek an arrest warrant.
- Destruction of evidence. A police officer may enter and secure a crime scene pending issuance of a search warrant when there is probable cause or when contraband is within a private area and there could be persons present who could destroy evidence. A protective sweep can be conducted for persons to "secure the premises" to prevent destruction of evidence. Once the emergency terminates, so does the doctrine of necessity. Once victims are located, aided, or rescued or suspects are arrested, the emergency search is over. If there is probable cause that evidence or contraband is still present, an officer must seek another Fourth Amendment basis (i.e., consent or search warrant) to search further.

A parolee is in *constructive custody* of the government after release from prison and is subject to conditions supervised by a parole officer. A parolee waives Fourth Amendment rights during this parole period. A *parole search* requires a trigger or reasonable suspicion of renewed criminal activity or violation of parole condition to be conducted by a police officer. When practical, it is recommended a police officer attempt contact with a parole officer for authorization to conduct a parole search. The parole officer reviews the reasonable suspicion information gathered by the police officer and makes an independent decision that the search is necessary to enforce parole conditions. If contact with a parole officer is impractical or unsuccessful, and a reasonable suspicion trigger otherwise exists, the search should be conducted. Case law supports parole searches under the foregoing circumstances.

A *probation search* is possible because of the supervised release of a probationer into the community with a search clause or Fourth Amendment waiver attached to probation conditions. A probation search may be conducted without a trigger or reasonable suspicion of renewed criminal activity. The purpose of a probation search is to ascertain whether the probationer is or is not complying with the terms of probation. Prior authorization from a probation officer is not required. A probation search can be routinely conducted by any law enforcement officer as long as the search is not conducted in an arbitrary or harassing manner.

Administrative searches are based on a compelling governmental interest embodied in statute or case law. Under these circumstances, the interests of society take precedence over the privacy interests of the individual. Administrative searches include searches in custodial institutions, booking searches, vehicle inventories, fish and game code enforcement, immigration and border inspections, U.S. Customs, airport and courthouse searches, and driving under the influence (DUI) sobriety checkpoints. Probation and parole searches also are forms of administrative searches.

There is no constitutional privilege to refuse to provide or to destroy evidence. With a legal seizure basis, an officer may use reasonable force to prevent the swallowing of contraband. Examples of reasonable force include verbal commands and physical restraint holds that do not involve pain compliance, choking, or restriction of the blood supply. Unreasonable force (force that shocks the consciousness of the court) is unlawful and will result in evidence suppression on due-process grounds. Examples of unreasonable force include choke holds, which cut off the air supply; carotid restraints, which cut off blood supply; striking the suspect; pain compliance holds; and verbal threats to use unreasonable force. Force that may be reasonable to overcome resistance to arrest or prevent the escape of a perpetrator would be unreasonable to prevent the swallowing of physical evidence.

If a suspect has swallowed evidence, stomach pumping or the administration of an emetic to induce vomiting can legally take place if the suspect expressly consents to such procedures. If the ingested substance presents a clear and immediate threat to the suspect's life as independently determined by medical personnel, recognized life-saving procedures may take place, including stomach pumping or the use of emetics. The physician may not act as an agent of the police. Evidence recovered fortuitously during this emergency procedure is admissible. Though it is legally possible to have a judge issue a search warrant for an emetic procedure, such circumstances are rare.

Taking a blood sample from a suspect involves bodily intrusion. A separate search and seizure basis is required in addition to the suspect's being lawfully under arrest. If a blood sample is needed as a biological control in a homicide, rape, or assault case, a police officer must obtain consent from the suspect or seek a search warrant from a judge for the seizure. This is because the suspect's blood type will not change, i.e., no exigency. If a blood sample is needed as "under the influence evidence" in a driving while intoxicated or vehicle manslaughter case, a police officer may seize the blood sample pursuant to exigency. This is because of the possibility of destruction of evidence. The alcohol or drug levels would metabolize in the suspect's body during the time it would take to seek a search warrant. Reasonable force may be used to take a blood sample from a resisting suspect. Police department policies differ on whether such force is to be used in misdemeanor cases. Unreasonable force is prohibited under due process and can result in evidence suppression. A blood sample can be taken from an unconscious "under the influence" suspect as long as there is reasonable cause to arrest.

There is no constitutional privilege to refuse to be fingerprinted or give exemplar evidence (e.g., handwriting, voice, photograph) incident to a lawful arrest. This evidence is nontestimonial in nature and does not violate a suspect's privilege against self-incrimination. An officer may use reasonable force to obtain such evidence, though the level of resistance by the suspect may well mitigate the quality of the exemplar evidence obtained. A resistant or uncooperative suspect should be advised that the suspect has no right to refuse to provide this evidence. Any refusal or resistance can be argued later in court as evidence of consciousness of guilt.

Methods of Identification

An *in-field show-up* is a viewing of a suspect by a victim or witness in the field soon after a crime is committed. The following are guidelines associated with show-ups:

- Contemporaneous. An in-field show-up can generally be conducted within 2 hours after a crime, although case law has extended this time frame to 24 hours in serious felony cases.
- Avoiding element of suggestiveness. A police officer bears the burden to show the identification transaction was controlled in a manner that prompted neutrality and avoided undue suggestiveness. Victims and witnesses should be separated before the interview and view the suspect or suspects separately. No suggestive remarks or showing of material objects should take place before viewing. Victims or witnesses should be given the admonition beforehand that they are under no obligation to identify, they should make no inference from the fact the suspect is in police custody or by a police car, it is just as important to free innocent persons from suspicion as it is to identify the guilty, and the witness should be positively sure of any identification.
- Fifth Amendment issues. A legally detained or arrested suspect has no right to refuse to participate in a show-up because such evidence is nontestimonial in nature. The suspect may be asked to repeat words or phrases uttered during the commission of a crime for voice identification for the same reason. There is no right to confer with counsel or have an attorney present during a show-up.
- Transportation during an in-field show-up. As a rule, if a suspect has been detained, the suspect cannot be moved for the purposes of accomplishing an identification. A victim or witness must be brought to the detention scene for viewing. Exceptions to this rule include situations in which the suspect is under arrest and consents to be moved, a victim or witness is injured or handicapped and it would be impractical for them to move, or there are other circumstances such as police officer safety, radio communication problems, or crime scene security that would justify moving the suspect.

A *photographic line-up* is an array of photographs shown to a victim or witness in an attempt to identify a suspect. It is important that the persons in the photographs be similar in physical description and background and that a victim or witness be given a cautionary admonition before viewing the line-up. A photographic line-up is generally performed well after a crime has occurred in which suspect information has been developed and an identification is part of the evidence needed to seek a criminal complaint and arrest warrant.

A *physical line-up* is a staged viewing in which a victim or witness looks at a number of persons in an attempt to identify a suspect. The persons must be of similar physical description and stature. If a criminal complaint has been filed against a suspect, the suspect has the right to have an attorney present during the viewing portion of the line-up. A physical line-up is generally conducted when a suspect is in custody and involved in several offenses or multijurisdictional crimes in which a number of victims or witnesses are present for identification purposes.

Miranda and Admissions or Confessions

The *Miranda rule* applies in the following situations:

1. For an adult, when the suspect is in custody and a police officer desires to interrogate to gain an admission or confession.
2. For a minor, when the suspect is taken into custody for a status offense, a delinquent offense, violating a court order, or escaping from a juvenile court-ordered commitment. Minors must be advised per Miranda contemporaneously with custody regardless of an officer's initial intent to interrogate.
3. The elements of the Miranda rights advisory apply only to criminal cases and include the following:
    *   The suspect can remain silent.
    *   Anything the suspect says can and may be used against him or her in a court of law.
    *   The suspect has the right to talk to a lawyer before or during questioning.
    *   If the suspect cannot afford an attorney, the court will appoint one to represent him or her free of charge before any questioning.

The suspect must make a knowing, voluntary, and intelligent decision to waive Miranda rights before any questioning. *Knowingly and intelligently* means the suspect has the mental capacity to be able to understand the choice in making a statement to the police and makes an informed decision to do so. Voluntarily means the waiver is free from coercion, inducement, promise, trickery, or submission to police authority. If the suspect asserts the right to remain silent, no questioning can take place. Exceptions include situations in which the suspect voluntarily initiates questioning on a separate and unrelated crime.

If the suspect asserts the right to speak to a lawyer, no in-custody, police-initiated questioning about the crime can take place. Exceptions are voluntary reinitiation of questioning on the part of the suspect or, if the suspect is released from custody, questioning on a separate and unrelated offense. Statements made in violation of the Miranda rule (or Sixth Amendment right to counsel) are inadmissible as evidence in court.

The Miranda rule *does not apply* in the following situations:

1. Contacts (consensual encounters). A Miranda warning is not required in everyday approaches, field interactions, or conversations with a person on the street or in a public place.
2. Traffic stops. A Miranda warning is not required during a traffic or municipal code infraction stop because there is no custody.
3. Detentions. A Miranda warning is not required during a temporary stop for investigation and questioning to determine a person's involvement, if any, in criminal activity. Even though a person's freedom of movement is seized during a detention, that person is not in custody for the purposes of Miranda unless they are handcuffed, secured in the rear of a police car, or their freedom of movement is otherwise restricted similar to an arrest. Though a person has the right to remain silent during a detention, the officer is under no legal obligation to tell the suspect about this right.
4. Rescue doctrine and public safety exception. The rescue doctrine is predicated on determining the health, safety, and whereabouts of a kidnap victim or stolen child or during false imprisonment, hostage, or other crime-victim situations. The purpose is to rescue the victim. The public safety exception involves asking questions to solve an exigency, such as the whereabouts of a gun, other dangerous instrumentality, bomb, clandestine lab, or hazardous materials that may have been abandoned or secreted by a suspect. The purpose is to abate a factual danger to life, limb, or property. In both instances, though a suspect may be in custody, questions may be asked absent a Miranda warning to resolve the exigency. If the suspect chooses to answer, responses may be used later in court.
5. General on-scene questioning. This involves on-scene questioning in the field or "knock and talk"–type questioning at a suspect's home whenever a police officer is in a "what happened?" or investigative mode. A Miranda warning is not required because no one is in custody.
6. Voluntary interview. This is similar to on-scene questioning and is usually a term reserved for station house interviews. The suspect is not under arrest, is free to leave at any time, is not required to answer any questions, and is informed of these conditions. A Miranda warning is not required, because although investigative questioning may take place, no one is in custody.
7. Telephone calls. A Miranda warning is not required during a telephone interview, because the person being questioned over the telephone is not in custody.
8. When a subject (suspect) is being questioned by someone other than a peace officer.

CIVIL (PRIVATE) LAW

Torts

Unlike a crime, which is an act or offense against society, a ~~tort is a civil wrong committed against a person or property~~, excluding breach of contract. The act, committed without just cause, may have caused physical injury, resulted in damage to someone's property, or deprived someone of personal liberty and freedom. Torts may be intentional (willful) or unintentional (accidental).

Examples of intentional torts include the following:

- Assault—the open threat of bodily harm to someone.
- Battery—any unconsented-to bodily contact. It may or may not result from the threat of assault.
- Wrongful death—causing another's death through reckless conduct.
- Defamation of character—damaging a person's reputation by making public statements that are both false and malicious. Defamation can take the form of libel or slander. Libel is expressing in print, writing, pictures, or signs or through publication, statements that injure the reputation of another. The words also can be read aloud by a speaker or broadcast for the public to hear. Slander is speaking defamatory, or damaging, words intended to prejudice others against an individual, jeopardizing the person's reputation or means of livelihood.
- False imprisonment—the unlawful violation of the personal liberty of another. The offense is treated as a crime in some states.
- Fraud—deceitful practices in depriving, or attempting to deprive, another of individual rights.
- Invasion of privacy—intrusion into a person's privacy, or private affairs, public disclosure of private facts about a person, false publicity about a person, using a person's name or likeness without permission.

Unintentional torts include situations involving negligence that occur when a person fails to exercise ordinary care and someone is injured. The accused may have failed to perform an act that a reasonable person in similar circumstances would perform or may have done something that a reasonable person would not do.

Most professional liability actions (commonly called malpractice suits) are based on an alleged act of negligence. All professional liability claims are classified on the basis of the word *feasance* which means "the performance of an act." Malfeasance is the performance of a totally wrongful and unlawful act. Misfeasance is the performance of a lawful act in an illegal or improper manner. Professionals can be legally accountable if their action or omission meets the four requirements necessary for the legal definition of negligence. Often referred to as the four Ds of negligence, they include the following:

- Duty. The person charged with negligence owed a duty of care to the accuser.
- Derelict. The provider breached the duty of care to the person.
- Direct cause. The breach of the duty of care to a person was a direct cause of the person's injury.
- Damages. There is a legally recognizable injury to the person.

The increased frequency of lawsuits is a concern to all professionals. To protect themselves against criminal or civil charges, professionals should practice good public relations with everyone, become familiar with relevant federal and state laws, make every reasonable effort to comply with those laws, and adhere to a professional code of ethics.

Contracts

A contract is a voluntary agreement between two parties wherein specific promises are made for a consideration. To be legally binding, the following four elements must be present in a contract:

1. The agreement. An offer is made and accepted. The contract stage is set with the making of an offer by one party to another. The offer, which relates to the present or the future, must be communicated, made in good faith and not under strain or as a joke, clear enough to be understood by both parties, and define what both parties will do if the offer is accepted. An offer may be revoked or withdrawn before acceptance. The acceptance must be absolute and in accord with the terms of the offer. If the acceptance includes conditions other than those made in the original offer, this constitutes a counteroffer for another contract. Mutual assent is part of the agreement and is evidenced by the offer and acceptance. For a contract to exist, both parties must understand the agreement in the same way and agree to the same terms and conditions.
2. Consideration. Something of value is bargained for as part of the agreement. When contracts are made, each party agrees to do or provide something for the other. This exchange of promises is called *consideration*.
3. Legal subject matter. The offer made in the agreement must be for legal services or purposes. Contracts are not valid and enforceable in court unless they are for legal purposes. For example, a contract entered into by a drug addict to pay for services of a drug dealer would be illegal. In this case, the contract would be void (set aside, as though it had never existed). Breach of contract may be charged if either party fails to comply with the terms of a legally valid contract.
4. Contractual capacity. Parties who enter into the agreement must be competent. If either of the concerned parties is incompetent at the time a contract is made, the agreement may be voidable. The option remains for the contract to be set aside or to be invalidated at a later date. Incompetent parties include the following:

- Minors. A minor is anyone younger than 18 years or the age of majority and not emancipated. Emancipated minors are individuals between the ages of 15 and 18 years who are married, in the armed forces, or self-supporting and no longer living under the care and control of their parents.
- Mentally incompetent. For a contract to be legal, the persons entering into the transaction must be capable of fully understanding all its terms and conditions. A person declared insane by the courts cannot enter into a legal contract. In some cases, mental incompetency extends to those under the influence of drugs or alcohol.

Types of Contracts

Contracts are expressed (explicitly stated in written or spoken words) or implied (unspoken contracts resulting from actions of involved parties). An expressed contract can be written or oral, but all terms of the contract are explicitly stated. In each state, the Statute of Frauds, derived from the "Statute for the Prevention of Frauds and Perjuries" formulated in England in 1677, states which contracts must be in writing to be enforced.

Third-party payor contracts fall under the Statute of Frauds. Any promise by a third party to pay for the services of another must be in writing to be enforced. Certain financial arrangements do not fall under the Statute of Frauds. However, they must be in writing according to Regulation Z of the Consumer Protection Act of 1968. This act is also known as the Truth-in-Lending Act. The agreement must be in writing and must contain the following items:

- Fees for services
- Amount of any down payment
- The date each payment is due
- The date of the final payment
- The amount of each payment
- Any interest charges to be made

The primary purpose of this legislation is to protect consumers from fraudulent, deceptive, or hidden finance charges levied by creditors. It can also be used by creditors to collect outstanding debts.

Implied contracts are implied if the conduct of the parties, rather than expressed words, created the contract. The contract is valid if both parties understand the offer, both are competent, and the services provided are legal.

REFERENCES

California Community Colleges. 1996. *Public safety curriculum and professional development project: Law enforcement curriculum.* Sacramento, Calif.: Chancellor's Office of the California Community College System.

Furriel, V. J. 1989. *California criminal law and criminal evidence.* Capistrano Beach, Calif.: Quik-Code Publications.

Hunt, D. D. 1998. *California criminal law concepts.* Edina, Minn.: Burgess International Group.

Judson, K., and S. Blesie. 1994. *Law and ethics for health occupations.* New York: Glencoe.

State of California. (1998) *Evidence Code.* §1–599.

State of California. (1998) *Penal Code.* §1–210.5.

Part Two

Components of Public Safety and Security

Chapter 4

Law Enforcement

HISTORY OF POLICING

For more than 20 years, the author has presented the history of policing in terms of eras, or periods of time (P. J. Ortmeier, lectures presented at University of Nebraska, 1976). These periods of time in police history also were addressed in a symposium held in 1997 at the John F. Kennedy School of Government at Harvard University (Lasley, Hooper, and Derry 1997).

Prepolice Era (Before the Early 1800s)

The prepolice period was characterized by self-policing. Protection of persons and property was the responsibility of individuals. Therefore, in a sense, security, or private policing, dominated this period. In communities such as villages and towns individuals took turns as nonpaid night watchmen. For the most part, there was no formalized public police service.

Amateur and Political Era (Early 1800s to 1930)

The amateur and political period in policing was characterized by urbanization, industrialization, migration of people, and growth in the public and private (security) police. In the United States, as well as the world, the development of a formalized police service was slow. Historians trace the beginnings of police departments to Detroit in 1801, Cincinnati in 1803, and the first federal investigative agency to the U.S. Post Office in 1828.

London, England, is often credited with having the first full-time paid public police department in the world. Largely as the result of the efforts of Sir Robert (Bobbie) Peel, the British Parliament, on September 9, 1829, passed the London Metropolitan Police Act. Sir Robert Peel believed that the practice of self-policing was no longer appropriate. He believed that as communities grew, it was necessary to have full-time, paid, professional police officers to prevent crime and apprehend criminals. Few organizational models of any type existed at the time. Those that did exist were structured along military lines. Therefore the military structure was adopted for the London Metropolitan Police. The officers were placed into a hierarchial rank structure and placed in uniforms similar to those of the military. Largely because of the fear of governmental interference with privacy, these new police officers were not very well accepted by the public at first. In fact, the new officers were nicknamed "Bobbie's boys," and the London Metropolitan Police are referred to as "bobbies" to this day.

In the United States, Chicago was credited with the development of a police department in 1837, Boston in 1838, New York City in 1844, San Francisco in 1847, and Dallas in 1856. At the Federal level, an investigative arm was formed in the U.S. Treasury Department in 1864, and the Border Patrol was established in the U.S. Department of Justice in 1882.

Private policing (or security) grew during this period as well. In 1850, Henry Wells and William Fargo established two cargo companies. One, namely American Express, operated east of the Missouri River. The other, Wells Fargo, operated west of the Missouri River. In 1851, Allen Pinkerton established the first private security company in the United States. The Pinkertons provided private police services to the railroads and detective services. Under contract during the Civil War the Pinkertons functioned as the intelligence arm of the Union Army. In 1858, Edwin Holmes introduced the first burglar alarms, and Washington Perry Brink introduced the first armored carriages for the transportation of money and valuables. In 1909, the Burns Security Agency was established to provide security for banks. Private police remained prominent during this period because of slow growth of public law enforcement.

Other significant dates and events during this period included the formation of the Los Angeles Police Department in 1869, the Philadelphia Police in 1885, the introduction of fingerprinting as an identification medium in St. Louis in 1904, and the formation of the Bureau of Investigation (forerunner of the FBI) in the U.S. Department of Justice in 1908. Between 1909 and 1932, August Vollmer, an innovative police chief in Berkeley, California, was the first to motorize police patrol, establish college courses for police officers, use psychological testing for police recruits, and create the first scientific crime laboratory in the United States.

In 1924, John Edgar Hoover was appointed director of the U.S. Department of Justice Bureau of Investigation. At the time of his appointment, the bureau was characterized by inefficiency and corruption. A career federal bureaucrat with no law enforcement experience, J. Edgar Hoover moved quickly to change the image of the bureau. Hoover improved standards, maintained strict discipline, added *Federal* to the bureau's name, and established the FBI as the preeminent law enforcement organization in the world.

Although public and private police agencies proliferated during the amateur and political period, policing remained primarily a local function controlled at the municipal level. The police, for the most part, were adjuncts to local political machines and were highly decentralized. In a sense, the police provided service to local political constituents and exercised a tremendous amount of discretion in the enforcement of the law. These services were provided through foot patrol and call boxes and were consistent with the desires of the local community. The outcome was high citizen satisfaction and social order, at least at the local level. The price paid for this satisfaction and social order was a tremendous amount of police corruption.

Reform Era (1930s through 1970s)

As a reaction to police corruption, President Herbert Hoover in 1929 appointed George Wickersham to chair the National Commission on Law Observance and Enforcement. Commonly referred to as the Wickersham Commission, its final written report was submitted and published in 1931. The commission made several recommendations to improve the quality of law enforcement and the administration of justice in the United States. The commission also recommended a college degree in liberal arts for police officers.

The reform era was depicted by a trend toward professionalism, state control, and civil service. Police agencies became *criminal law enforcement* agencies that focused more on apprehension than crime prevention. "Other" duties of the police, such as fire fighting and medical emergency response, were transferred to fire and medical emergency units. The goal of crime control was viewed as the main job of the police. Discretion was limited, and policing was "removed" from the people to reduce the possibility of corruption. Policing became isolated and impersonal as the result of motorization, specialization, and bureaucracy.

Between 1929 and 1939, private security declined as a result of the Great Depression. Between 1940 and 1945, because of World War II, the use of private security increased. After World War II, professionalism in law enforcement and private security grew because many returning veterans, who had acquired military police experience during and immediately after the war, selected police work and private security as an occupation. In 1954, George Wackenhut, a retired FBI agent, formed what was to become the third largest private security company in the U.S.

During the reform era, police work became standardized, and police training programs were established. California in 1959 established the Commission on Peace Officer Standards and Training (POST). The use of technology to fight crime increased and preventive patrol and rapid response to reported crime and calls for service became a priority. However, the crime rate continued to increase throughout the 1960s and 1970s. Antiwar protests, campus unrest, and the civil rights movement challenged the police.

In 1967, another national commission was established to investigate the nature and extent of crime in the United States and develop recommendations for the improvement of the criminal justice system. The President's Commission on Law Observance and Administration of Justice, commonly referred to as the President's Crime Commission, essentially replicated the efforts of the Wickersham Commission in 1931. Its recommendations focused on improvement in the quality of law enforcement, court services, and corrections. Unlike the federal government's response to the Wickersham report, this time Congress acted and in 1968 passed the Omnibus Crime Control and Safe Streets Act. As a result, the federal government budgeted billions of dollars to fight crime. Among its provisions, the act established the Law Enforcement Assistance Administration (LEAA) in the U.S. Department of Justice. This bureaucracy was responsible for channeling federal dollars to local, county and state governments to establish and improve police training programs and to upgrade equipment and facilities. A major portion of the federal dollars were earmarked for the Law Enforcement Education Program (LEEP). This program provided grants and interest-free loans to preservice and in-service law enforcement personnel to attend college. Colleges and universities throughout the country became eligible for federal funding that enabled them to establish college-level education programs in law enforcement and criminal justice.

Significant trends during the reform era included the increased role of women in law enforcement and the growth in private policing. Although women had been working in law enforcement since the early 1900s, it was not until the 1960s that women assumed patrol responsibilities traditionally performed by their male counterparts. Women first worked as patrol officers in Indianapolis, Indiana, in 1968. Contrary to early beliefs, studies have revealed that there is no appreciable difference in performance between a female officer and her male counterpart. Women also appear to be more effective in handling domestic disputes. Private security also continued to grow. In fact, the number of people employed and expenditures for private security in 1970 had reached approximately the same level as that found in public law enforcement.

Despite the federal effort and marked improvements in the quality and quantity of police services, the crime rate continued to increase between 1968 and the early 1970s. As a result, a third major national commission was formed in the early 1970s to, once again, investigate the nature and scope of crime in the United States. The National Commission on Criminal Justice Standards and Goals to a great extent replicated the efforts of the Wickersham Commission in 1931 and the President's Crime Commission in 1967. One of its last reports, the Task Force Report on Private Security, was published in 1976. For the first time, a national commission recognized private security as an essential component of public safety. The task force recommended that the private sector be encouraged to improve the nature and quality of security services to complement the law enforcement community in its efforts to fight crime and reduce the crime rate. Thus the 1970s created an environment in which private security began to assume a more responsible role in the crime fighting and prevention effort.

In the 1960s and 1970s, police community relations emerged as a concern because of the social unrest resulting from antiwar demonstrations and urban riots. Communities experimented with the concept of team policing, which involved a reorganization of traditional police forces into integrated and versatile police teams assigned to fixed districts. Team policing represented an attempt to reconnect the police with the public to enhance police-community relations.

Community Problem-Solving Era (1980s to Present)

From the early 1980s to the present, policing has involved a gradual return to citizen and community involvement in the policing effort. This period is characterized by a need for information critical to solving problems within the community. Police strategies therefore focus on eliminating the barriers that isolate the police from the public and reducing the isolation that developed during the reform era.

In an effort to reconnect the police with the public, many departments throughout the country experienced a rebirth of community policing in the 1980s. Community policing may be defined as "a philosophy and a strategy which promotes community engagement, participation, and problem solving; action which leads to the discovery and implementation of solutions to community problems" (Ortmeier, 1996). Community policing is based on the assumption that the community and the police are one entity. A community involved with the police in the identification of community problems and solutions to those problems is more effective than one that is not. Communities tend to receive the type of police service they support, and this community support is vital to successful policing. In addition, the police public image depends on the public's confidence in the integrity of the police and on the judgment exercised by individual police officers.

Crime prevention and problem solving during this era are viewed as important as crime fighting. In 1994, Congress passed, and the president signed, a new $32 billion crime bill. Even though the crime rate had been declining since the early 1990s, the crime bill was the federal government's response to citizen fear of crime. Essentially, this federal solution to the crime problem was very similar to the Omnibus Crime Control and Safe Streets Act of 1968, which had little impact on crime reduction. In fact, the crime rate continued to increase after implementation of the 1968 provisions. As discussed in Chapter 1, law enforcement, in and of itself, may have little appreciable impact on crime. However, crime may be reduced significantly when the police work with, and receive support from, the community.

During this period, the security industry continued to grow rapidly because of limited law enforcement resources. By 1991, 580,000 people were employed in public law enforcement and 1,500,000 persons were employed in private security. By the year 2000, it is estimated that private security personnel will outnumber law enforcement personnel four to one.

JURISDICTIONAL LEVELS

Law enforcement is a function of the executive branch of government. For example, although sheriff's deputies or county marshals may be assigned to provide security to state courts and U.S. marshals provide security in federal courts, these sworn officers fall under the jurisdiction of the executive rather than the judicial branch of government.

Law enforcement in the United States is highly decentralized. It is estimated that the number of separate and distinct law enforcement jurisdictions in the United States may be close to 20,000. This would include agencies of the federal, state, county, and local government. It would also include villages that have a single town marshall as well as cities with large police departments.

National (Federal) Law Enforcement

National law enforcement agencies have broad territorial jurisdiction and narrow subject-matter jurisdiction. This means that federal agents have authority to operate anywhere in the United States or its territories but are limited in the types of laws they may enforce. Virtually every department of the U.S. government contains a law enforcement component. What follows are the names of several of these departments with a partial listing of the types of agencies and agents contained in each.

1. U.S. Department of Justice
   - Federal Bureau of Investigation (FBI)
   - Immigration and Naturalization Service (INS)
     - Border Patrol
     - Immigration inspectors
   - Drug Enforcement Administration (formerly the Bureau of Narcotics and Dangerous Drugs)
   - U.S. Marshall's Service
2. U.S. Department of the Treasury
   - Secret Service
   - Internal Revenue Service (IRS)
     - Revenue agents
     - Internal Security (Internal Affairs)
     - Special agents (Criminal Intelligence Division)
   - U.S. Customs Service
     - Customs inspectors
     - Special agents (criminal investigators)
   - Bureau of Alcohol, Tobacco and Firearms (ATF)
   - International Criminal Police Organization (Interpol). Not an actual police agency, Interpol is a clearing house for information on international criminals; the U.S. liaison to Interpol is housed in the U.S. Department of the Treasury.
3. U.S. Department of Labor
4. U.S. Department of Agriculture
5. U.S. Department of Defense
   - Military police, investigators, intelligence

6. U.S. Department of the Interior
   - Park police
   - Park rangers
7. U.S. Postal Service
   - Postal inspectors
8. General Services Administration
   - Federal protective officers
9. U.S. Department of Transportation
   - U.S. Coast Guard

State, County, and Local Law Enforcement

Most policing in the United States is a state, county, and local function. The jurisdiction of state, county, and local law enforcement agencies essentially is the reverse of that of federal agencies. Whereas federal agencies have very broad territorial jurisdiction, state and local agencies have very narrow territorial jurisdiction, that is, their authority is limited to the boundaries of the municipality, county, or state. On the other hand, police agencies confined within state boundaries have very broad subject-matter jurisdiction, that is, they enforce a wide variety of state and local laws.

State agencies include the state police and the state highway patrol. Some states have one or the other, and a few states have both. Although officers in both types of agencies have full peace officer powers within the state, the state police are typically responsible for policing state government property and providing executive protection for the governor. The primary responsibility of state highway patrol agencies is traffic law enforcement. The Texas Rangers are credited with being the first state police agency.

The chief law enforcement officer for a county is the sheriff. The sheriff and the sheriff's deputies provide law enforcement services throughout the county and may, in many jurisdictions, staff county jails. The sheriff typically patrols rural and unincorporated areas of the county as well as municipalities that do not possess their own police departments.

Local, or municipal, police departments provide police service to villages, towns, and cities. These agencies typically confine themselves to the city limits and are headed by a chief who is politically appointed by the mayor, city council, or a police commission. In some cities that have a department of public safety, the police chief may be provided with civil service protection.

ROLE OF STATE, COUNTY, AND LOCAL POLICING

The police are the community; the community is the police. Although the police are most often viewed as separate from the community, they are actually a part of the community and reflect the community's values. Studies have shown that a given community receives the type of police service it desires and supports. Community support is absolutely essential to efficient and effective policing.

Weaknesses in the link between the police and the public may be attributed to three primary causes. These include apathy and indifference displayed by the public toward the police, open hostility by many toward police, and increasing charges of police brutality, true or not. Most people base their opinion of the police on what they hear and see in the news and entertainment media or on personal experience as a criminal offender, traffic violator, or victim of a crime. Therefore virtually all contact between the public and the police tends to be negative. Furthermore, most people believe that crime reduction is the responsibility of the police rather than the entire community. Citizens, therefore, are reluctant to assume responsibility for crime prevention or crime reduction.

Official Police Functions

Official police functions fall into three broad categories. These include enforcement of the criminal law (the crime-fighting function), maintenance of order (the peace-keeping function), and service-related activity. The general public's image of the police is that of crime fighters. However, most police officers' time is not spent fighting crime; the police spend most of their time keeping the peace, regulating noncriminal conduct, and responding to calls for service. In fact, most officers may not use their firearms, except at the firearms range, in their entire career.

The Organization of Police Agencies

At the state, county, and municipal levels, police organizations are typically organized into three broad categories. These include administrative, auxiliary, and line services. Administrative services include training, personnel, planning and research, legal matters, community relations, and internal affairs. Auxiliary services include communication, record keeping, data processing, supply and maintenance, laboratory facilities, and temporary detention. Line services include patrol, investigation, traffic control, specialized units such as special weapons and tactics (SWAT), sting operations, vice control, and drug enforcement.

The backbone of any police department is patrol operations. The purposes of police patrol include crime prevention, detection and apprehension of criminals, traffic law enforcement, emergency response, and community assistance and service. Types of patrol include foot, vehicle, bicycle, mounted horse patrol, motorcycle, airborne, and marine.

SKILLS AND QUALITIES OF THE LAW ENFORCEMENT OFFICER

The skills and qualities needed by a law enforcement officer include the following:

1. Technical skill. The officer must develop skills relative to defensive tactics, weapons, and procedures.
2. Communication. Oral and written (report writing) skills are critical. The saying, "Paper is our most important product!" is especially important in police work.
3. Human relations. This is the most important consideration for effective police work and effective police-community relations. Good relations between the police and the public equate with more and better cooperation regarding budgets, reporting crime, and supplying information to the police.
4. Leadership. The position and status of law enforcement in the criminal justice system make it the most visible component of the system. The police therefore are in a position to assume a leadership role in the community.
5. Cognitive skill (knowledge). The police officer must know the elements of law and evidence.
6. Judgment. Police officers must be able to exercise effective judgment in split-second decision making.
7. Attitude. One of the most important qualities of a law enforcement officer involves attitude. If a police officer's attitude consistently demonstrates isolationism, gestapo tactics, and verbally abusive language toward all people, the officer and the department of which the officer is a part will be unable to generate the community support necessary for effective and efficient policing.
8. Integrity. This is probably the most important quality for a police officer. Adherence to a standard of ethics inspires trust and trust is the primary ingredient in effective police–community relations.

POLICE STRATEGY AND TACTICS

Several studies conducted over the past 25 years call into question the effectiveness of some police strategies and tactics. These studies have dealt with the effectiveness of preventive patrol, officer safety and productivity, domestic disturbances, the role of the uniformed officer in investigations, citizen fear of crime, and rapid response. A brief description of the results of these studies follows.

Preventive Patrol

A study focused on the effectiveness of preventive patrol was conducted by the Police Foundation in Kansas City in the early 1970s. Commonly referred to as the

Kansas City Preventive Patrol Experiment, the results of the year-long study were published in 1974. During the study, the city was divided into fifteen areas. Each area was designated to receive one of three levels of patrol activity. In some areas, the district was saturated with patrol cars in a proactive attempt to maintain high visibility. In other areas, patrol activity was decreased and patrol cars entered the area only when there was a call for service. In other areas, patrol activity remained unchanged. The results of the study were startling. They indicated that there is little appreciable difference in crime rates between areas that are patrolled heavily and those that are not. It was also interesting to note that most police activity was citizen initiated. Rarely does a police officer on patrol see a crime committed. The results implied that considerable cost savings could be realized, without a commensurate increase in crime, if random preventive patrol was diminished. In addition, a study conducted by Sparrow, Moore, and Kennedy in 1990 indicated as much as 80 percent of a patrol officer's time is uncommitted and 95 percent of dispatched calls may not require immediate response.

Officer Safety and Productivity

One-officer patrol cars are as safe and productive as two-officer cars. Except where backup is often necessary, officers may be safer, more productive, and more cost effective if assigned to one-officer units.

Domestic Disturbances

Arresting, rather than counseling, assailants in domestic disputes may be more effective in reducing the likelihood of repeat assaults.

Role of Uniformed Police in Follow-up Investigations

A study conducted by the Rand Corporation in 1977 concluded that detective units solve only a small portion of crimes. If uniform police officers carefully gather information after the commission of a crime and communicate it to detectives and the detectives actually use the information, detective productivity increases. The results of the study indicated that uniform patrol officers should become more actively involved in follow-up criminal investigations.

Fear of Crime

Police methods that increase the quantity and improve the quality of police-citizen interaction reduce citizen fear of crime. Less citizen fear of crime equates with more citizens on the street, which results in prevention of additional crime.

In nonemergency situations, citizens appear to be satisfied with alternatives (e.g., telephone counseling, delayed response) to rapid response. A study in Newark, New Jersey, in 1981 concluded that although foot patrol does not necessarily reduce crime, it does reduce citizen fear of crime and increase officer satisfaction.

Rapid Response

Police strategy throughout the latter half of the twentieth century has focused on rapid response to crime reports under the theory that offenders may be more readily apprehended. However, studies such as the one conducted in Kansas City, Missouri, in 1978, have shown that citizens may wait 20 to 40 minutes before calling the police. Therefore, rapid response may not result in an increase in the number of apprehensions.

ISSUES AND PROBLEMS IN POLICE WORK

Officer Safety and Survival

The number of police officers killed in the line of duty in 1996 dropped dramatically to the lowest level since 1960, a decline that experts say is at least partly attributable to the decrease in crime in many big cities in the United States. One hundred seventeen federal, state, and local law enforcement officers were killed in the line of duty in 1996, a 30 percent drop from the 162 officers who died in 1995, according to the National Law Enforcement Officers Memorial Fund in Washington. Over the past 10 years, the average number of officers killed was 166. The last time the figure was as low as 117 was in 1960, before the jump in violence that signaled the beginning of modern America's crime wave.

Most police officers are killed or injured during four types of incidents—effecting arrests, robbery and burglary in progress calls, domestic disturbances, and vehicle stops. Studies have shown that police weapons themselves are hazardous to officers. Statistics imply that a police officer is just as likely to be killed accidentally with a police weapon as by an armed robbery suspect. Deaths of and injuries to police officers often can be traced to errors on the part of the officers themselves. P. R. Brooks outlined ten of these deadly errors in his book, *Officer Down: Code Three.* They include the following:

1. Poor attitude. If a police officer fails to pay attention to the job, errors will soon be made. It can cost the police officer and fellow officers their lives.
2. Tombstone courage. No one doubts that officers are macho. In any situation in which time allows, the police officer must wait for backup. There are few instances in which, alone and unaided, a police officer should try to make a dangerous apprehension.

3. Not enough rest. For police officers to do the job, they must be alert. Being sleepy or asleep on the job is against regulations and it places police officers and the community in danger.

4. Taking a bad position. A police officer should never allow anyone being questioned or about to be stopped to get into a better position than the police officer or the police vehicle. There is no such thing as a routine call or stop.

5. Danger signs. Police officers learn to recognize danger signals. Suspicious movements and strange cars are examples of warnings that should alert a police officer to watch and approach with caution. A police officer should know the beat and the community and watch for what is out of place.

6. Failure to watch the hands of a suspect. Is the suspect reaching for a weapon or getting ready to strike the police officer?

7. Relaxing too soon. Getting into the "rut" of believing all alarms are false or accidentally set off may lead to complacency. A police officer should observe the activity and never consider any call routine or just another false alarm.

8. Improper use of or no handcuffs. Once a police officer has made an arrest, the prisoner should be properly handcuffed.

9. No search or poor search. There are so many places to hide weapons that a police officer's failure to search is a crime against fellow officers. Many criminals carry several weapons and are able and prepared to use them against police officers.

10. Dirty or inoperative weapon. Is the police officer's weapon clean? Will it fire? How about the ammunition? When did the police officer last qualify with a weapon? What is the sense of carrying any firearm that might not work?

The Psychological Dynamics of Police Work

It is estimated that only 10 percent of the population of the United States has the psychological profile necessary to be a police officer. Studies also demonstrate that possibly as many as one third of those currently employed in law enforcement do not fall within the 10 percent. Police work itself tends to determine police behavior. Education and training apparently have little effect. Education does, however, enhance communication, human relations, and problem-solving skills. Police departments that have high educational levels tend to have fewer lawsuits filed against the department for police misconduct.

Police officers tend to become cynical because of the element they deal with. Officers develop a subculture that may be used as a mechanism for self-protection. As time goes on, officers may become alienated and isolated from virtually everyone in the community. Certainly, the police view the criminals as the enemy. The courts and lawyers who appear to protect defendants and citizens who complain eventually may also become the "enemy." As the stress associated with the job spills over into the officer's personal life, relationship problems with family and friends may develop. Problems in relationships are the leading stressor among police officers, and the relationship problems are directly attributable to the officer's "taking the job home." Seventy-five percent of police officers end up divorced.

Eventually, the authority to use force becomes personalized, and an unruly suspect is seen by an officer as an affront to the officer's authority. The police are sworn to enforce the law, and many police officers tend to interpret the law strictly. Respect for authority is reinforced by the job itself, and the police tend to enforce the law according to its letter rather than its spirit.

Discretionary Enforcement

The model for most police organizations is a military operation. Both the police and the military commonly wear uniforms, have a definite rank structure, carry lethal weapons, and possess the authority to use force as necessary. However, military personnel are typically submerged in a unit and operate under direct supervision. Police officers, on the other hand, are rarely subject to the direct control of a supervisor. Therefore police officers may be in a position to exercise enormous amounts of discretion with respect to the enforcement of the law. An individual police officer's personal views with respect to the law itself may dictate behavior. An officer also may choose to enforce the same law against one person but not another. Complaints of racism and abuse often result. Studies have shown, however, that the perceived social class of the individual, not race, determines treatment received by police officers. Studies also have shown that in cases in which citizens complain of abuse by the police, both the officer and the citizen allegedly abused are of the same race.

Some laws are enforced rigorously while others are not. Depending on community demands, the police may select to enforce certain types of laws, for example, those relating to prostitution, because the community or neighborhood demands strict enforcement. The public itself may dictate police behavior and styles of police service. A community receives the type of police service it supports, desires, or tolerates. In *Varieties of Police Behavior*, James Q. Wilson described three styles of police behavior. Under the watchman style, the police view themselves or are viewed as community caretakers. Under the service style, the police are expected to provide a wide range of services to the community. Under the legalistic style, the police are viewed as a militaristic force responsible for near full enforcement of the law.

Use of Force

Excessive use of force by police officers has become a critical issue. Incidents such as that in Los Angeles with Rodney King that are viewed by the public through the news media portray law enforcement as an aggressive and abusive occupying army. Police use of force actually is dictated by the circumstances rather than the type of crime. Contrary to common belief, the police nationally may be involved in fewer than 3,000 shooting incidents per year. Police use of deadly force usually occurs at night, in public places, and in high-crime areas of large cities.

Police Corruption

Although rare in contemporary policing, bribery, extortion, and political favors are a constant threat in police work. Police officer Frank Serpico uncovered pervasive, organized corruption in the New York City police department in the 1960s. The Los Angeles police department was an extremely corrupt organization in the 1920s and 1930s. Because of the nature of the business, the temptation to engage in corrupt activities and benefit financially are always present. Certainly one would not argue against the assertion that bribery is not only corrupt but also criminal. Some would argue that accepting a gratuity of any kind is inappropriate. Carried to the extreme, some may argue that acceptance of free coffee by a police officer is gratuitous behavior.

Violation of Rights

The Bill of Rights, the first ten amendments to the U.S. Constitution, originally applied only to the national government. However, through the use of the due-process clause of the Fourteenth Amendment and a doctrine of selective incorporation, the U.S. Supreme Court has selectively applied provisions of the first ten amendments to state, county, and local law enforcement. Many of the decisions impacting law enforcement were an outgrowth of the Warren court years during the 1950s and 1960s, when Earl Warren was chief justice of the U.S. Supreme Court. During this period, the high court applied provisions of the following amendments to state and local governments:

- Fourth Amendment—search and seizure issues and the application of the exclusionary rule
- Fifth Amendment—freedom from double jeopardy and self-incrimination. The due-process clause in this amendment applies to federal law enforcement agencies.
- Sixth Amendment—right to a speedy trial, right to trial by jury, right to an attorney, and right to face accusers
- Eighth Amendment—no excessive, cruel, or unusual punishment
- Fourteenth Amendment—due-process clause that applies to state law enforcement agencies

Liability Issues

A serious concern for the police and law enforcement administrators in recent years has been the development of a liability connection between the agency, individual officers, and civilian complainants. Litigation arising from several types of situations and incidents has been costly in terms of dollars and in terms of the image of the police. Litigation of this nature typically arises from four areas—excessive use of force, deaths and injuries resulting from pursuit driving incidents, sexual harassment, and discriminatory practices. Studies have indicated that police departments with high education levels tend to have fewer lawsuits filed against them and their officers.

Investigation of Domestic Abuse

Violent crime within a family, assault, and even murder are often the end result of a long history of domestic conflict. In fact, in domestic homicides the police have often made a previous call to the home. The police typically are caught in the middle and are placed in a precarious position. Police responses and styles of control in domestic abuse situations generally fall into the following four categories: penal, which involves arrest; compensatory, which involves persuading one person in the dispute to make restitution to the other; therapeutic, which involves providing help to the disputants; and conciliatory, which involves seeking a settlement in the dispute. Police responses may depend on the situation and the discretion of the officers.

When responding to a domestic abuse call, officers must consider their own safety as well as the safety of the victim. They also must evaluate the injury to the victim. In many states, domestic abuse is not a felony unless there is serious visible injury. Some states, however, are developing stricter laws. In California, for example, any visible injury or nonvisible injury indicated by the victim's complaint is sufficient to establish probable cause for a felony arrest.

In some cases, restraining orders are in effect. If the suspect abuser is present, a misdemeanor is being committed whether the "victim" consents to the suspect's presence or not. A victim cannot consent to a violation of criminal law. If the suspect is not present, a crime report should be taken. In some states, notably Texas, the victim of domestic abuse may be arrested for failure to provide the identification of the perpetrator.

In domestic disturbance situations in which an arrest is not warranted, the law often does not prescribe the officer's actions. In these cases, officers should approach with caution, separate the disputants, use distracting techniques, identify the problem, and assist the disputants in arriving at a solution. If possible, officers should refer the disputants to community service agencies such as medical services, social services, welfare, child protective services, and counseling services.

Limited Resources

The budgets of law enforcement agencies have become increasingly strained. Competition for tax dollars, governmental and political priorities, and the

increasing cost of public police personnel and equipment have limited the ability
of the police to keep pace with the demand for law enforcement services. Eighty
percent of the nation's police departments have fewer than a dozen sworn
officers.

Public police agencies could save time and money by establishing complementary relations with private security organizations. Many security companies
and agencies possess technology and resources that surpass those of local police
counterparts. Private security also can extend the eyes and ears of the police by
collecting and offering information, extended surveillance, and investigatory services. Their vital role played in crime prevention should not be overlooked by the
public police either. As cited in the National Advisory Commission on Criminal
Justice Standards and Goals Task Force Report on Private Security in 1976, the
private security professional may be the one person in society who has the
knowledge and technology to effectively prevent crime. The public police cannot
be everywhere at once. Private agencies can fill the gap, and public agencies
would do well to cooperate with the private sector and promote improved training of security personnel to upgrade the quality of security services.

REFERENCES

Bocklet, R. 1990. Police–private security cooperation. *Law and Order* 38 (December):
    54–59.
Brooks, P. R. 1975. *Officer down: Code three.* Schiller Park, IL: Motorola Teleprograms,
    Inc.
Coffey, A. 1990. *Law enforcement: A human relations approach.* Englewood Cliffs, N.J.:
    Prentice-Hall.
Cunningham, W., J. J. Strauchs, and C. W. Van Meter. 1990. *Private security trends 1970
    to 2000: The Hallcrest report II.* Boston: Butterworth-Heinemann.
Goldstein, H. 1990. *Problem-oriented policing.* New York: McGraw-Hill.
Inciardi, J. A. 1996. *Criminal justice.* 5th ed. San Diego: Harcourt Brace College
    Publishers.
Lasley, J. R., M. Hooper, and G. M. Derry III. 1997. *The California criminal justice system.*
    Upper Saddle River, NJ: Prentice-Hall.
Meese, E., III. 1993. Community policing and the police officer. *Perspectives on policing
    no. 15.* Washington, D.C.: National Institute of Justice.
Meese, E., III, and A. T. Kurz, Jr. 1993. Community policing and the investigator. *Journal
    of Contemporary Criminal Justice* 9 (December): 289–302.
National Advisory Commission on Criminal Justice Standards and Goals. 1976. *Report of
    the Task Force on Private Security.* Washington, D.C.: U.S. Government Printing
    Office.
Ortmeier, P. J. 1995. Educating law enforcement officers for community policing. *Police
    and Security News* 11 No. 4 (July–August): 46–47.
Ortmeier, P. J. 1996. *Community policing leadership.* Ann Arbor, Mich.: UMI Dissertation
    Services.
Schmalleger, F. 1997. *Criminal justice: A brief introduction.* 2nd ed. Upper Saddle River,
    N.J.: Prentice-Hall.

Souryal, S. 1977. *Police administration and management.* St. Paul, Minn.: West Publishing.
Sparrow, M. K., M. H. Moore, and M. Kennedy. 1990. *Beyond 911.* New York: Harper.
Wilson, J. Q. 1968. *Varieties of police behavior: The management of law and order in eight communities.* Cambridge: Harvard University Press.

Chapter 5

Courts

The courts are the pivot upon which the legal system turns. Probably no other single component of public safety or the criminal justice system impacts the other components or society in a more significant way. The courts determine guilt or innocence, adjudicate civil litigation, and issue decisions that impact the process through which criminal and civil cases pass. An enormous amount of discretion is exercised in the judicial process. Furthermore, because of court delays and the lengthy nature of many trials, the judicial process is slow. As a result, court processes in the United States are largely administrative, whereby cases are settled through negotiated pleas rather than through adversarial processes as they were originally intended to be.

HISTORY

Each of the American colonies had its own court system. The Massachusetts Bay Colony formed a combined legislature and court in 1629 to make laws, conduct trials, and impose sentences. By 1639, county courts were established, and the original court formed in 1629 served primarily to hear appeals.

By 1776 all American colonies had established court systems. After the American Revolution, the colonial courts provided the basis for development of state court systems. By the late nineteenth century, the growing population, the settlement of the west, and the movement toward urbanization led to an increase in civil lawsuits and criminal arrests. To service the need, legislatures passed laws that created numerous courts and a variety of court structures. Federal courts were established by the U.S. Constitution, the Judiciary Acts of 1789 and 1925, and the Magistrate's Act of 1968. Since the early 1900s, court systems in the United States have become more uniform and streamlined. The federal court system is three tiered, and state court systems generally include three or four tiers of courts.

COURT SYSTEMS AND STRUCTURE

The U.S. Constitution specifically makes provision for only one court, the U.S. Supreme Court. Article III, Section 1 of the Constitution reads, "the judicial power of the United States shall be vested in one Supreme Court, and in such inferior courts as the Congress may from time to time ordain and establish." It was the Judiciary Act of 1789 that created other federal courts, namely the U.S. District Courts and U.S. Circuit Courts of Appeal. State courts were established by state constitutions and state statutes. There are at least fifty-five separate and distinct court systems in the United States and its territories. They include the federal system, fifty state systems, and one system each in the District of Columbia, Guam, Puerto Rico, and the U.S. Virgin Islands. If all the separate courts operating within these systems were totaled, the number would exceed ten thousand.

There are two basic types of courts—trial courts and appellate courts. Trial courts are where trials, whether criminal or civil, take place. Appellate courts, with rare exception, do not "try" cases. Rather, they hear appeals brought before them from the trial courts. Appeals from trial courts proceed through either a state or federal appellate review process and culminate at the U.S. Supreme Court.

FEDERAL COURTS

United States Supreme Court

The U.S. Supreme Court has original (or trial) jurisdiction in very rare cases involving foreign ambassadors, public ministers, or when a state is a party to an action. In an overwhelming majority of cases, the U.S. Supreme Court functions as an appellate court. It reviews constitutional challenges to federal and state statutes and appeals from criminal and civil trial court cases brought before it through state appeals courts and the U.S. Court of Appeals. The U.S. Supreme Court also has the power to bypass the appellate review process and reach down through the system to bring a case before it. In these cases, the Supreme Court issues a writ of certiorari to order the lower court to forward the case to the high court. In addition, the Supreme Court may occasionally respond to a question of law certified to it by a U.S. Court of Appeals.

In most cases, the U.S. Supreme Court hears appeals (grants certiorari) from the lower courts. However, the Supreme Court does not hear all appeals brought before it. The right of review of lower federal court rulings by the U.S. Supreme Court are enumerated in Article III, Section 1 of the U.S. Constitution. With respect to state court judgments, appeal is only a matter of right when the validity of a federal statute is questioned in a state court or when a state statute is challenged as repugnant to the U.S. Constitution. In addition, with respect to review of state court judgments, the following rules apply:

1. There must be a substantial federal question involved. The Supreme Court will not review cases if there are adequate and independent state grounds for disposition of the cases.

(2) The petitioner must have exhausted all state appellate procedures. (Exception: habeas corpus proceedings in which violation of an individual's rights under the U.S. Constitution is an issue.)

(3) The state judgment must be final. (Exception: freedom of speech and irreparable injury cases.)

The U.S. Supreme Court has no authority to make a final determination in a state case. The Supreme Court may affirm (agree with) the decision of the lower court or reverse (disagree with) the decision and remand (return) the case to the lower court for a decision not inconsistent with the majority opinion of the U.S. Supreme Court. If the constitutionality of the entire state court proceeding is at issue, the charge against a defendant in a criminal case must be dismissed. If only certain evidence is declared inadmissible, the state court may order a new trial based on admissible evidence only. (Note: Trying the defendant a second time does not violate the Fifth Amendment double jeopardy clause because there has not been a final judgment in the case.)

Except in rare cases in which review of lower court decisions by the U.S. Supreme Court is a matter of right, review by the Supreme Court is discretionary on the basis of the self-imposed rules of the Court for selection of cases. These rules were outlined in an opinion issued in 1936 in the case of *Ashwander v. the Tennessee Valley Authority.* Commonly referred to as the Court's doctrine of judicial restraint, these rules include the following:

1. The U.S. Supreme Court will not pass on the constitutionality of a legislative act that is brought before the court in a friendly, nonadversarial proceeding.
2. The U.S. Supreme Court will not "anticipate" a question of constitutional law in advance of the necessity of deciding it.
3. The U.S. Supreme Court will not formulate a rule of constitutional law broader than is necessary as applied to the precise facts of the case at hand.
4. The U.S. Supreme Court will not pass on constitutionality if there is some other ground on which the case may be disposed, such as an adequate and independent state ground.
5. The U.S. Supreme Court will not pass on the validity of a statute on the complaint of one who fails to show injury.
6. The petitioner must not have benefited from the statute the petition seeks to have declared unconstitutional.
7. On validity of acts of Congress, the U.S. Supreme Court will first ascertain whether a construction (interpretation) of the statute is available by which the constitutional question may be avoided.

U.S. Courts of Appeal

The intermediate appellate courts in the federal system are the U.S. Courts of Appeal. Known as Circuit Courts of Appeal until 1948, the decisions of these courts are usually final except through the certiorari process to the U.S. Supreme Court. The U.S. Courts of Appeal have appellate jurisdiction over all U.S. District Court decisions except as follows:

1. When a three-judge district court has enjoined (stopped) enforcement of a federal or state statute on grounds of unconstitutionality; it then goes to the U.S. Supreme Court.
2. When a District Court declares a federal statute unconstitutional and the United States is a party to the action.
3. On a showing that a case requires immediate settlement because of imperative public importance.

U.S. District Court

The U.S. District Court is the trial court of general jurisdiction in the federal system. It has original (or trial) jurisdiction over civil actions on copyrights, patents, postal problems, civil rights, and almost all other civil and criminal cases arising under the laws and treaties of the United States and the U.S. Constitution. The U.S. District Court has concurrent jurisdiction with the states with respect to criminal cases in which a criminal act violates federal as well as state law. It has jurisdiction over civil cases in which the dollar amount in dispute is $10,000 or more and in which parties to the action are residents of different states.

U.S. Magistrates and Other Specialized U.S. Courts

U.S. Magistrates have authority to issue federal warrants, set bail, hold preliminary hearings in federal cases, and hold summary trials for minor federal crimes when the defendant waives the right to a trial in the U.S. District Court. Other specialized federal courts include the U.S. Court of Claims, which hears financial suits against the United States, the U.S. Court of Customs and Patent Appeals, the U.S. Tax Court, and the U.S. Court of Military Appeals.

STATE AND LOCAL COURTS

State and local courts are established by individual state legislatures and state constitutions. They hear criminal and civil cases arising out of incidents occurring within the state and violations of state and local laws.

State Court of Last Resort

Each state has a court of last resort for cases heard in, and appealed from, lower state courts. These courts are usually referred to as state supreme courts. Appeals from these courts are taken directly to the U.S. Supreme Court, the highest court in the United States.

State Intermediate Appellate Courts

Almost all states have some form of intermediate appellate court. They serve essentially the same function with state cases in a state court system that the U.S. Court of Appeals does with federal cases in the federal system.

State Trial Courts

State trial courts fall into three categories. They are referred to as trial courts of general, limited, or special jurisdiction. Courts of general jurisdiction may try any state criminal or civil case brought before them. Courts of limited or special jurisdiction are restricted in their authority. These courts typically try misdemeanor cases and conduct preliminary hearings in felony cases. If as the result of the preliminary hearing the court determines that probable cause exists to hold the defendant on the felony charge, the defendant is bound over to the court of general jurisdiction for arraignment and trial. Examples of courts of limited or special jurisdiction include municipal, juvenile, and small claims courts.

PRETRIAL PROCESSES

Criminal Cases

Pretrial processes in criminal cases typically proceed through the following stages:

1. **Arrest.** Initiation of the pretrial process in a criminal case is made through a physical arrest, issuance of a citation (summons to appear) in lieu of arrest, or issuance of an arrest warrant. A summons, which includes a notice of the charge and an order to appear in court, is issued in lieu of arrest for minor offenses.
2. **Booking.** Once arrested, an arrestee is booked. Essentially this involves the official recording of the arrest in the records of the arresting law enforcement agency. The arrestee is usually fingerprinted and photographed.
3. **Initial incarceration.** If the arrestee cannot be released on recognizance (ROR) without a bail hearing, and if a magistrate or judge is not immediately available, the arrestee may be detained in a jail or lock-up until a first appearance.
4. **First (initial) appearance.** Before a judge or magistrate, the accused is informed of the charge and advised of rights under the U.S. Constitution. Bail

is set, if possible. If the offense is minor, the accused may be allowed to waive a trial and plead guilty at this stage.

5. Indictment or information. In federal criminal cases, the formal charge against the accused must be issued by a federal grand jury in the form of an indictment. In state cases, the prosecuting attorney (district attorney) may take the case before a state grand jury for possible indictment or file an information, which is a formal charge issued from the office of the prosecuting attorney.

6. Preliminary hearing. The accused may waive the right to a preliminary hearing and plead guilty. If the right is not waived, the accused is again informed of the charge and rights under the U.S. Constitution. The preliminary hearing is conducted to determine whether probable cause exists to hold the accused on the charge and bind the defendant over for trial. During this hearing the prosecution must establish *prima facie* case, that is, on the face of the evidence presented by the prosecution, probable cause exists that a crime occurred and the defendant committed the offense in question.

7. Arraignment. Unless the offense is minor, the arraignment provides the first opportunity for a person to answer to a criminal charge. The answer is in the form of a plea. (In California, arraignment occurs before the preliminary hearing.)
   - Guilty. Most often, the defendant pleads guilty, either to the original charge or to an amended charge arrived at through a plea bargain.
   - Not guilty. A date and time are set for the trial.
   - No contest (nolo contendere). This plea is not an admission of guilt, but the defendant will not contest a declaration of guilt by the court (judge). An advantage to a no contest plea is that because it is not an admission of guilt, the defendant's plea cannot be used against the defendant in a subsequent civil proceeding.
   - Stand mute. In U.S. criminal jurisprudence, a defendant cannot be forced to say anything. Therefore if a defendant stands mute, a not guilty plea is entered by the court, and a trial date is set.

8. Pretrial motions. If the defendant is proceeding to trial, the defense attorney may file pretrial motions to do the following:
   - Have the charges dismissed
   - Suppress prosecution evidence as inadmissible
   - Discover what evidence the prosecution has
   - Delay the trial
     Dilatory tactics may benefit the defense because evidence may be misplaced and witnesses' memories may fade.

9. Jury selection. According to the U.S. Supreme Court, the Sixth Amendment guarantee to a jury trial applies to the federal government and to state cases in which the potential penalty for the crime charged is 6 months or more in jail or prison. The jury always functions as the finder (trier) of fact. Although the U.S. Constitution does not provide for a specific number of jurors, traditionally twelve persons make up a trial jury. Some states allow a six-person jury for offenses that are minor.

The initial list of potential jurors is selected from a list of registered voters or in some states from the list of those who hold driver's licenses. From the initial list, a jury pool (venire) of approximately three hundred people is selected. From the jury pool, a jury panel of approximately thirty people are referred to the court for jury selection. At the trial court, members of the jury panel are interviewed by the judge, prosecution, and defense during a voir dire (to speak the truth) examination to determine their suitability for hearing a trial.

Potential jurors may be excused as the result of a challenge for cause or because of a peremptory challenge. Challenges for cause are unlimited. However, peremptory (no cause need be given) challenges are limited in number. If the appropriate number of jurors and alternates cannot be selected from the thirty jury panel members, the bailiff or clerk of the court is asked to return to the jury pool for additional candidates for the jury.

Once a trial jury is selected, the jury is sworn in (impaneled), and the trial begins. To avoid being influenced by outside publicity, the jury may be sequestered. While sequestered, jury members are not allowed to communicate with each other or the outside world regarding the trial.

Civil Cases

Pretrial proceedings in civil cases typically include the following:

1. Complaint filed by plaintiff. Plaintiff files papers claiming a civil wrong by the defendant (respondent).
2. Answer by the defendant (respondent). Defendant files papers denying plaintiff's claim and stating the defense in the case.
3. Pretrial proceedings. Motions (requests by the parties to the court) are filed requesting discovery (an exchange of information and facts between the parties).
4. Jury selection. Selection follows a procedure similar to that followed in criminal proceedings.

TRIAL PROCESSES

The following is a short explanation of the steps in either a criminal or a civil trial:

1. Opening statement by plaintiff or prosecutor. The plaintiff's attorney (in civil cases) or the prosecutor (in criminal cases) explains to the trier of fact the evidence to be presented as proof of the allegations (unproven statements) in the complaint, indictment, or information.
2. Opening statement by defense. The defendant's attorney explains evidence to be presented to deny the allegations made by the plaintiff or prosecutor.

3. Direct examination of witnesses for the plaintiff or prosecutor. Each witness for the plaintiff or prosecution is questioned. Other evidence (e.g., documents, physical evidence) in favor of the plaintiff or prosecution is presented.
4. Cross-examination of witnesses by the defense. The defense has the opportunity to question each witness. Questioning is designed to attack the credibility of (impeach) the witness in the mind of the trier (finder) of fact (jury or in a non-jury trial, the judge).
5. Motions. If the prosecution or plaintiff's basic case has not been established from the evidence introduced, the judge can end the case by granting the defendant's motion to dismiss or by entering a directed verdict.
6. Direct examination of witnesses for the defense. Each defense witness is questioned.
7. Cross-examination of the witnesses by the plaintiff or prosecution. Each defense witness is cross-examined.
8. Closing statement by plaintiff or prosecution. Plaintiff's attorney or prosecutor reviews all the evidence presented (noting uncontradicted facts), states how the evidence has satisfied the elements of the charge, and asks for a finding of guilty (in criminal cases) or for the plaintiff (in civil cases).
9. Closing statement by defense. Similar to closing statement by prosecution or plaintiff, except the defense asks for a finding of not guilty (in criminal cases) or for the respondent (in civil cases).
10. Rebuttal argument. Prosecutor or plaintiff has the right to make additional closing arguments.
11. Jury instructions. Judge instructs the jury about the law that applies in the case.
12. Jury deliberations. These deliberations are not public, and the jury may be sequestered.
13. Verdict. In most states, a unanimous decision is required one way or the other. If the jury cannot reach a unanimous decision, it is said to be a hung jury, and the case may be tried again.

POSTTRIAL PROCESSES

Criminal Cases

If a defendant is found not guilty, the defendant is released. Not guilty verdicts cannot be overturned or reversed. If the defendant is found guilty, the judge typically orders a presentence investigation to be conducted by the probation department. At sentencing, the judge may impose a fine, jail, prison, probation, suspended sentence, or, in some states, execution. Postconviction remedies for the defendant include appeal and habeas corpus when all other appeal remedies are exhausted.

Civil Cases

In civil cases, the respondent (defendant) may appeal or move to have the judgment set aside.

COURT DELAY

The results of public opinion polls regarding the courts indicate general displeasure with the courts and court delays. Some people believe that violation of the law is even encouraged by the courts. Complaints against the courts may be addressed through an exploration of the reasons why U.S. courts appear to have lost control of their workloads. These reasons include the following:

Why are they behind and backed up?

1. Independence of the U.S. judiciary. One of the charges leveled against King George III in 1776 in the Declaration of Independence was that he made the judiciary dependent on him. As a result, Americans have sought to make the judiciary independent of the executive and the legislative branches of government. Therefore, American courts are largely immune from executive management and legislative control.
2. Lack of administrative talent within the judiciary. Law school curricula are not designed to prepare graduates for administrative work. Instead law students study the law and judicial decisions. Therefore managing caseloads does not receive a high priority in the courts.
3. Other constraints on court management. The goal of the courts is individual justice in individual cases. If independent judgment is to be preserved, administrative procedures that may influence judgment should be avoided. In addition, the judiciary is not a pyramid of authority running from top to bottom. Rather it resembles a cadre of scholars at a university who are expected to work together as colleagues.

IMPACT ON PUBLIC SAFETY AND SECURITY

Decisions from the courts have a tremendous impact on the other components of the public safety and security system. Some decisions are viewed as positive, whereas others appear to have a negative impact on the ability of public safety and security personnel to accomplish admirable goals. Reversed convictions, civil judgments, high litigation costs, and the development of procedural law and rules of evidence often are viewed negatively by those who have been given the task of protection of persons and property. Over an extended period, however, it would appear that common good may be achieved through adherence to the constitutional principles that established the United States as a republic. Public safety and security personnel are more effective as agents of protective services if adherence to constitutional principles are the top priority.

REFERENCES

Law Enforcement Assistance Administration (1976). *Two hundred years of American Criminal Justice.* Washington, DC: U.S. Government Printing Office.
Schmalleger, F. 1997. *Criminal justice today.* Upper Saddle River, NJ: Prentice Hall.

Chapter 6

Corrections and Juvenile Justice

THE CORRECTIONAL PROCESS

The key points in the correctional process have hardly, if ever, been analyzed in total because decisions regarding the correctional client are made at each point by specialists from vastly different organizations. The specialists include the police, prosecutors, defense attorneys, judges, probation officers, jail and prison personnel, and parole officers. The only person who has contact with all phases of the process is the offender.

The pretrial period is actually the port of entry into the correctional process. This period is crucial to prevention of future offenses because the likelihood of repeat offenses increases the longer the offender remains in the system. In addition, the consequences of any detention may have a negative impact on the offender's family, job, and social relations. Families may become dependent on public assistance, and the total cost of incarceration may increase dramatically. During the trial period, the offender may be led to believe that the system can be manipulated through negotiations and plea bargaining. In addition, defense attorneys, prosecutors, judges and juries make decisions that have long-term consequences.

If a defendant is found guilty, the posttrial period may involve any combination of fines, jail, probation, prison, and in some cases, the death penalty. The offender becomes labeled or marked for life as a convicted offender. The label often negatively affects the offender's self-concept and may result in repeat offenses. During the postincarceration period, an offender is expected to reintegrate into society. However, incarceration and exposure to the system enhance the problems associated with reintegration. The offender may be a different person because of personal problems and personality shifts that develop during extended stays in a security-conscious setting. At release, the offender is expected to be self-sufficient and responsible in the community rather than passive and obedient.

PHILOSOPHIES IN CORRECTIONS

Throughout history, several philosophies have developed with respect to corrections. Each essentially involves a set of assumptions and a rationale for corrections. A brief summary of these philosophies follows.

Retribution

Retribution is based on the concepts of revenge and vengeance. Expiation, or suffering and punishment, is the central theme. In theory, the offender should associate pain with wrongdoing and seek to avoid pain by demonstrating legally acceptable behavior.

Deterrence = legitimate goal

Deterrence operates under a theory that punishment in and of itself may operate to deter future criminal activity. Through the concept of *general deterrence*, it is assumed that punishing a person will deter others from committing similar offenses. Through *specific deterrence*, it is assumed that punishment will deter the individual offender from committing another offense.

Incapacitation = making it so they are incapable of doing it again

Incapacitation involves rendering the offender incapable of repeated offenses. Isolation of the offender through institutionalization in a jail or prison removes the offender from society, incapacitating the offender from victimizing members of an open community. Other forms of incapacitation, rarely if ever used, include chemical castration or total isolation in a maximum security facility.

Rehabilitation

In a medical analogy, *rehabilitation* implies that there are identifiable causes of crime and that these causes may be treated and cured. The philosophy also implies that the offender is capable of rehabilitation even though the correctional client may not have had the ability to conform behavior to the requirements of the law in the first place. Rehabilitation is one of the dominant philosophies in corrections today.   *very low success rate

→ *only truly possible with the strength of Jesus Christ

Reintegration

- assimilating back into society + making a positive contribution

Most persons who enter the correctional system eventually are discharged and released from custody. It is hoped that through exposure to the correctional process, the correctional client returns to society and does not reoffend. The true measure of success in corrections may lie in reintegration.

INSTITUTIONAL CORRECTIONS

At any given time, approximately one third of all correctional clients are institutionalized. The typical institutions are jails and prisons.

Jails

Municipal or county jails are facilities under the local control of the chief of police or county sheriff. In some areas the jails have been separated from the sheriff, and the county maintains a separate department of corrections. Jails house inmates awaiting trial or serving sentences of 1 year or less. Because of the short length of stay, effective vocational education or counseling programs are practically nonexistent. Overcrowding in jails has become a major problem.

Prisons

Prisons at the state and federal level house convicted offenders who are serving long sentences. In 1790 Philadelphia's Walnut Street Jail became the first American prison. Often referred to as a Pennsylvania-style system, it promoted segregation and isolation of prisoners from each other. In 1823, a prison was established in Auburn, New York. The Auburn model promoted congregate labor and communal eating facilities with little segregation. Most prisons in the United States adopted the Auburn model.

Prisons are classified as minimum, medium, or maximum security facilities, and inmates are assigned to each depending on their level of dangerousness and escape risk. Various security levels may exist within a single institution. Securing prisoners is a primary function of prisons. Many prisons offer several programs. These programs may include treatment and counseling for physical, psychological, and chemical abuse problems; work-related activities, such as prison industries and work-release programs; vocational training; educational programs, such as high school and college; and religious programs. Inmates, or residents, in prisons are classified according to their custodial (security) needs, program needs, and type of offense. In some states, inmates also are classified according to their level of maturity.

Problems and issues in prisons are many and varied. Often the need to secure the inmate population conflicts with the desire for effective treatment. Control and supervision of residents to prevent escapes, disorder, and the introduction of contraband is the primary focus of prisons. Problems associated with sexual behavior also develop. Nonconsensual homosexual behavior increases in prisons.

To prevent such behavior and as a reward for good behavior, a few institutions permit conjugal visits between inmates and their spouses.

Prisons develop subcultures and inmate social systems. Institutionalization, or prisonization, develops as inmates internalize the values and norms of the inmate population. In some cases, inmates become more criminal in their behavior. Studies have shown that the rehabilitative effect of incarceration reaches a peak at about 18 months and declines thereafter. Therefore the impact of treatment in prisons appears to have little effect on the recidivism rate because as many as two thirds of all inmates released from prison commit repeat offenses and return to prison.

Disorder in prisons due to homosexual assaults, racial conflict, and disturbances is commonplace. Extreme disorder may manifest itself in riots and deaths of inmates and staff. Overcrowding is a problem that is predicted to worsen. California's already crowded prisons are projected to add 57,700 inmates by 2003, a 37 percent increase. In 1997, the state's adult prisons housed 155,687 prisoners, compared with 66,965 in 1987. Officials predict the population will reach 202,855 in 2002 and 213,420 in 2003.

Three Strikes Legislation ✕

incapacitate

In recent years, lawmakers at the state and federal levels passed legislation that provides for severe penalties for those convicted repeatedly of serious offenses. The public's fear of crime and the belief that many offenders are released too soon have led many jurisdictions to enact three-strikes laws to remove recidivists from society for long periods of time, in many cases for life. Between 1993 and 1995, twenty-four states and the federal government enacted three-strikes laws.

Washington and California were the first states to enact three-strikes laws. In Washington, all three strikes must be for felonies specifically listed in the statute. Under California law, only the first two strikes need be from the state's list of strikeable offenses—*any* subsequent felony can count as a third strike. California's law also contains a two-strikes provision under which a person convicted of any felony who has one prior conviction for a strikeable offense may be sentenced to twice the term the person would receive otherwise.

The long-range impact of three-strikes legislation is uncertain. Preliminary studies indicate it may have an impact in reducing the crime rate, although it has little effect on prison crowding.

NONINSTITUTIONAL CORRECTIONS

Approximately two thirds of all correctional clients are not institutionalized. Most sentences involve a fine or exposure to some form of community-based correctional program.

increased use due to expense, overcrowding, and burden on CJ system

Diversion and Community Service Programs

In some cases, a correctional client may be diverted from the criminal justice system entirely. These programs provide early intervention for first-time offenders when the offense is minor. Offenders who successfully complete a diversion program may not acquire a criminal conviction record. Types of programs include detoxification, youth activities, and civil commitment to public or private treatment facilities. In other cases, the offender may be sentenced to complete a community service activity, such as roadway litter removal or other public works. These types of programs produce the additional benefit of reducing operating costs for the correctional component of the criminal justice system.

Probation

(before incarceration)

Although a part of the correctional process, probation is a function of the courts. It usually involves a sentence of conditional release to the community without jail or prison time. Exceptions include shock probation programs in which first-time offenders are incarcerated briefly to give them exposure to jail. Properly administered probation programs, with recommended probation officer caseloads of thirty to forty clients, tend to have high success rates. However, actual caseloads may be well over one hundred. The likelihood of receiving probation depends to a great extent on the presentence investigation and recommendation made by the probation officer. Probationers who violate a condition of probation may be returned to the sentencing court for reevaluation. Typical violations include additional criminal activity or leaving the jurisdiction without permission.

Parole

(after incarceration)

Most prison inmates eventually are released from prison either after completion of their full sentence or on parole. Parole is a function of the prison system and involves a form of conditional release from a state or federal prison facility. As with probation, parole officers typically have heavy caseloads, and effective supervision of parolees is difficult. Most sentencing laws provide for early release from prison if the inmate follows a prescribed course of treatment and is not involved in misconduct while incarcerated. Commonly referred to as good-time laws, these laws provide for up to a 50 percent reduction in time served in prison.

The origins of parole in the United States can be traced to the early nineteenth century. Problems associated with overcrowding, discipline, security, and the effectiveness of rehabilitation led to the use of parole as a means of encouraging positive behavior within prison populations. The first notable effort to provide some flexibility in prison sentences was the 1817 New York State good-time law. In 1837, Massachusetts passed the first comprehensive parole law in the United States.

Other Community-based Programs

Community-based corrections is a term often used to refer to noninstitutional correctional programs, including diversion, half-way houses, probation, and parole. In its broadest contest, however, community-based corrections involves a wide variety of community resources that may be utilized to assist and "treat" an offender. These resources include social and health services, work and study release programs, counseling, and chemical abuse programs.

CAPITAL PUNISHMENT

Aside from any moral issue or societal retribution associated with a court-ordered execution, two major questions remain. Does the death penalty operate as a deterrent to crime? Do the benefits of execution outweigh the costs? An execution certainly is a specific deterrent in that the offender who is put to death will not reoffend. However, does the possibility of the death penalty operate as a general deterrent that prevents murders from occurring in the first place? The evidence suggests that few individuals reflect on the possibility of execution before killing another human being.

The second major question surrounding the death penalty involves the cost. According to a 1997 Department of Justice report, the average cost of incarcerating an individual for 50 years is approximately $1 million dollars. However, the cost of an execution, if the costs associated with appeals and an average stay of 9 years on death row are included, approaches $2 million dollars!

In the 1930s, approximately 200 people were executed in the United States each year. Between 1930 and 1967, there were 3,859 executions, 60 percent of which took place in 17 southern states. Thirty-three were federal executions. The rate of executions began to decline in the 1950s. The last federal execution occurred in 1963. Between 1967 and 1977, no one was executed in the United States. The Eighth Amendment to the U.S. Constitution provides that there shall be "no cruel or unusual" punishment. In a sense, the death penalty almost became unconstitutional because it had not occurred in 10 years and was therefore an unusual occurrence.

In 1972, in the case of *Furman v. Georgia,* the U.S. Supreme Court struck down many death penalty statutes. Because a disproportionate number of persons in minority groups were being executed, the court held that the death penalty was cruel and unusual and therefore in violation of the Eighth Amendment, because it was being applied in a discriminatory manner. Many states rewrote their death penalty statutes to conform to the new U.S. Supreme Court guidelines. On January 7, 1977, a rebirth of the death penalty occurred in Utah with the execution of Gary Gilmore by a firing squad. In 1995, 3,054 prisoners were under the sentence of death and 56 executions occurred in 16 of the 37 states that still have death penalty statutes.

JUVENILE JUSTICE

Public safety and security personnel encounters with juveniles are often problematic because juvenile behavior is frequently legally ambiguous. Behavior that might be unacceptable for a mature adult is, nevertheless, acceptable within a juvenile peer group. For example, juvenile gangs may stake out turf in a public area and designate it as their private space because they have nowhere else to go. Public safety personnel must balance the law, neighborhood and community practices, and the image of authority without under- or overreacting to a situation.

Problems with juveniles typically fall within two categories—delinquency and dependency. *Delinquency* is involved when a youth commits an act that would be classified as a crime if committed by an adult. *Dependency* issues arise when a child has been neglected, sexually abused, or battered. Under the principle of *parens patriae,* the state, acting in place of the parents and usually through a juvenile or other county court, may step in to act on behalf of the child. The adjudication process focuses on disposition in the best interests of the child rather than conviction for a crime.

In recent times, serious problems have developed with juvenile gangs. Gang types include the following:

* Informal hedonistic groups motivated by pleasure or rebellion against authority
* Culture- or ethnicity-based groups motivated by loyalty toward, and protection of, each other
* Predatory or instrumental groups motivated by economic opportunity and power

Public safety and security personnel should realize that not all juvenile gangs are involved in criminal behavior. Likewise, many crimes are committed by juveniles who are not members of gangs. Police agencies in the United States made an estimated 2.7 million arrests in 1995 of persons younger than 18 years. In 1995, for the first year in nearly a decade, juvenile arrests for violent crime index offenses declined 3 percent. Even with this decline, the number of juvenile violent crime arrests in 1995 was 12 percent greater than the level in 1991 and 67 percent above the 1986 level.

In 1997 an expert panel was convened by the U.S. Department of Justice, Office of Juvenile Justice and Delinquency Prevention to study serious and violent juvenile offenders. The panel concluded the following:

- Serious and violent juvenile offenders are a distinct group of offenders who tend to start early and continue late in their offending.
- From childhood to adolescence, serious and violent juvenile offenders tend to develop behavior problems, including aggression, dishonesty, commission of property offenses, and conflict with authority figures.
- Many potential serious and violent juvenile offenders younger than 12 years are not routinely processed in juvenile court, and services in the community for such offenders appear unnecessarily fragmented, leading to a lack of public accountability for young potentially serious and violent juvenile offenders.
- Many known predictors of serious and violent juvenile offending could be incorporated into screening devices for the early identification of serious and violent juvenile offenders.
- It is never too early. Prevention intervention for young children at risk for becoming serious and violent juvenile offenders is known to be effective and should be implemented at an early age.
- It is never too late. Intervention and sanctions for known serious and violent juvenile offenders can reduce their risk for reoffending.
- Evaluations of interventions often are inadequate and usually do not provide specific information about changes in the rate of offending by serious and violent juvenile offenders.
- An integrated and coordinated program of research is needed on the development and reduction of serious and violent juvenile offending.
- Several key issues about serious and violent juvenile offenders are unresolved and must be addressed through research.

Other recent findings regarding juvenile crime include the following:

- Juveniles were involved in 32 percent of all robbery arrests, 23 percent of weapons arrests, and 15 percent of murder and aggravated assault arrests in 1995.
- Juveniles younger than 15 years were responsible for 30 percent of juvenile violent crime arrests in 1995, but they accounted for more than half (55 percent) of the decline in these arrests between 1994 and 1995.
- Juvenile murder arrests declined 14 percent between 1994 and 1995. The number of juvenile arrests for murder in 1995 was 9 percent below the level in 1991, but still 90 percent above the number of murder arrests in 1986.
- In contrast to violent crime, juvenile property crime index offense arrests showed no change between 1991 and 1995.
- Juveniles were involved in 13 percent of all drug arrests in 1995. Between 1991 and 1995, juvenile arrests for drug abuse violations increased 138 percent.
- Arrests of juveniles accounted for 14 percent of all violent crimes cleared by arrest in 1995.

The juvenile justice system faces unprecedented challenges. Although juvenile arrests for violent crime have declined in recent years, the current level of arrests is not acceptable. Today's juveniles do not commit more violent crime than juveniles a generation ago, but more juveniles are violent. Juvenile arrestees are more likely than adult arrestees to use a gun when committing a crime. Juveniles are most likely to commit violent crimes after school, and half of all high school students who carry a weapon take the weapon to school.

Juveniles not only are the perpetrators of a great deal of crime but also often are victims of crime. Between 1985 and 1995, nearly 25,000 juveniles were murdered in the United States. The number of children identified as abused or neglected nearly doubled between 1986 and 1993. In the mid 1990s the rate of violent victimization of juveniles 12 through 17 years of age was nearly three times that of adults.

Juvenile criminal activity and victimization will remain a major concern for all public safety and security administrators. Although the juvenile crime rate appears to be declining in many areas, an increase in the number of juveniles in the beginning of the twenty-first century may produce an increase in juvenile crime. Because juveniles often are victims of crime perpetrated by other juveniles and by adults, a strategy must be developed to protect the generations of the future.

REFERENCES

Clark, J., J. Austin, and D. A. Henry. 1997. "Three strikes and you're out": A review of state legislation. *National Institute of Justice Research in Brief.* Washington, D.C.: U.S. Department of Justice, Office of Justice Programs.

Foote, J. 1997. *Expert panel issues report on serious and violent juvenile offenders.* Washington, D.C.: U.S. Department of Justice, Office of Juvenile Justice and Delinquency Prevention.

Gilliard, D. K., and A. J. Beck. 1996. Prison and jail inmates, 1995. *Bureau of Justice Statistics Bulletin.* Washington, D.C.: U.S. Department of Justice, Office of Justice Programs.

Sickmund, M., H. N. Snyder, and E. Poe-Yamagata. 1997. *Juvenile offenders and victims: 1997 update on violence.* Washington, D.C.: U.S. Department of Justice, Office of Juvenile Justice and Delinquency Prevention.

Snyder, H. N. 1997. Juvenile arrests, 1995. *Juvenile justice bulletin.* Washington, D.C.: U.S. Department of Justice, Office of Justice Programs, Office of Juvenile Justice and Delinquency Prevention.

Stephan, J. J. 1997. Census of state and federal correctional facilities, 1995. *Bureau of Justice Statistics executive summary.* Washington, D.C.: U.S. Department of Justice, Office of Justice Programs.

Chapter 7

Security Services

Security, according to the dictionary, is defined as freedom from danger and harm or something that secures or makes safe. In contemporary society, safety and security are a concern for every individual, family, group, public agency, or private enterprise. As discussed in Chapter 4, the origins of security can be traced to pre–law enforcement and public safety times when private individuals and groups assumed the responsibility for protecting themselves and their property. Formalized public safety and law enforcement organizations did not develop until the early nineteenth century.

In an organizational sense, contemporary security, as a function as well as a responsibility, is a thread woven throughout the operation of all public agencies and private institutions. As a function within any organization, security management (also known as loss prevention, asset protection, and risk management) may be defined as a public or private service-related activity or industry that provides personnel, equipment, policies, procedures, or a combination of these elements to prevent or reduce losses caused by human error, emergencies, human-made and natural disasters, and criminal action. More specifically, security provides personnel for emergency response, access control, deterrence, investigations, and protection of persons and property. Security also provides equipment for access control, surveillance, and fire protection. It provides policies and procedures for disaster recovery, emergency management, fire prevention, security education, and prevention of losses from any source.

Management is responsible for the safety and security of persons and property. If an organization has a security problem, it has a management problem. The business of security is global and universal. As such, it involves government, nonprofit and for-profit institutions. In a sense, security provides all protective services not performed by public law enforcement agencies. Several professional organizations focus on the business of security. Most notably, the American Society for Industrial Security (ASIS) is represented by close to 30,000 members in the United States and numerous foreign countries.

As the crime rate in the United States increased throughout the 1960s, 1970s, and 1980s, and law enforcement resources became increasingly strained, the security industry grew at an extremely rapid rate. In 1970, the number of security personnel in the United States, approximately 500,000, was roughly equivalent to the number in public law enforcement. By 1991, the number of police officers had increased to 580,000, and the number of security personnel increased to 1,500,000. By the year 2000, it is estimated that whereas the number of police officers may increase to 680,000, security personnel may number 2,000,000. Private security outspends public law enforcement by 73 percent. Private security clearly is the primary protective service in the United States.

Salaries for security managers and directors are competitive with those in public law enforcement and other corporate business enterprises. The results of a salary survey conducted in 1997 by the trade journal *Access Control and Security Systems Integration* indicated that the average salary for security directors is $72,190; 22.5 percent of the survey respondents placed their salaries at more than $100,000 per year. Security manager salaries were placed at $44,820 to $51,110. Operations-level security personnel salaries averaged $33,650 annually.

THE ROLE OF SECURITY IN GOVERNMENT AND BUSINESS

The ultimate goals of security are (1) establishment of a safe and secure environment and (2) loss prevention resulting in maximum return on the investment of public or private dollars. To reach these goals, security departments and organizations provide personnel, equipment, policies, and procedures to prevent or reduce loss from any source. Security is a multifaceted and strongly interdisciplinary occupational specialty. It generally involves criminal and civil law and investigations, business management, public policy, psychology, sociology, and technological advancements. Contemporary security operations specifically focus on fraud, disaster recovery, crime, energy management, substance abuse, fire prevention and protection, Internet violations, information protection, workplace violence, pre-employment screening, executive protection, terrorism, economic espionage, and safety.

Security is involved in, and interacts with, every aspect of public safety. It is involved with law enforcement in the crime prevention effort, interacts with the judicial system to assist in prosecution, and, through a trend toward privatization of certain correctional services, may be involved in the staffing and management of jails and prisons. The mission of private security also includes protection from and transportation of hazardous materials as well as fire safety and fire fighting (through industrial fire brigades). Security operations also may be used to generate revenue through the sale of products and services and may cut costs through entrepreneurial ventures and articulation arrangements with other security service providers.

Challenges for security management in the electronic age include protection of proprietary information of business and government agencies. Competitive pressures, foreign and domestic, combined with the ability to invade an institution (or country) electronically pose enormous threats to national security and modern government and business enterprise. Regardless of the cost associated with the development and implementation of an *effective* total security program, studies have demonstrated that the cost of security measures are offset by a reduction in future losses.

TYPES OF SECURITY ORGANIZATIONS

Security organizations may be categorized into four types—contract, proprietary (in house), hybrid, and virtual. The type of organization depends to a great extent on the situational needs of the agency or business of which the security operation is a part.

Contract Services

Contract organizations provide security services to other organizations for a fee. With the trend toward outsourcing and temporary employment services in the United States, contract security services have become increasingly popular. Contract services generally cost less and relieve the contractee of the administrative and legal responsibilities associated with pre-employment screening, management, and personnel supervision. There also may be disadvantages. These include the possibility of high turnover and low quality of personnel, disloyalty to the contractee, and a lessor degree of control over contract employees.

The types of security services provided under contract include guards, patrol, alarms, armored delivery, consultants, executive protection, pre-employment screening, drug testing, and investigative services. With respect to investigations alone, contractors may provide services and specialties in areas such as criminal defense, personal injury, surveillance, expert testimony, worker compensation, insurance fraud, hazardous waste disposal, undercover operations, trademark infringement, stalking prevention, personal protection, and executive protection.

Proprietary Security

Proprietary security organizations operate within and for a parent agency, business, or institution. Often referred to as in-house operations, these security units provide services similar to those offered by contract providers. The main difference is the employee-employer relationship. In a proprietary operation, security personnel are employees of the organization in which they actually work and are not under contract with a third-party agency or business.

Hybrid Security Organizations

Some security operations incorporate contract and proprietary personnel and benefit from the advantages of both. These hybrid security organizations employ a permanent proprietary security staff. They also employ contract security to supplement in-house operations. Virtually all large airlines, for example, employ a behind-the-scenes in-house security staff. They also employ a contract service to staff the x-ray equipment used to screen passengers, visitors, and carry-on packages before admittance to aircraft boarding areas.

The Virtual Security Organization

Some agencies or businesses may not have stand-alone security departments. The security function may be integrated or merged in other departments, such as human resources, health and safety, environmental services, and risk management. Economic conditions and budgetary constraints associated with consolidation, downsizing, or right-sizing may force a merger of a security component with another operational unit within an institution. As a function, security necessarily crosses departmental lines. With advances in technology, security virtually becomes an integral part of every facet of the entire enterprise.

FUNCTIONAL COMPONENTS OF SECURITY

Security operations may be categorized according to the functions they perform. These functions include the following.

Physical Security

Physical security involves mechanical loss prevention. It includes all tangible objects, such as walls, fences, locks, and building design, that promote the physical protection of persons and property. It also involves security personnel devoted to access control activities.

Personnel Security

Personnel security involves *protection of* as well as *protection from* persons. Typically associated with employees within an agency or business, personnel security also involves hiring the right people and maintaining their integrity. It involves the use of an effective pre-employment screening process and policies and procedures to reduce the opportunity and motive for employee theft and decreased productivity.

Information Security

Information is intangible, and the actual impact of information loss is difficult to measure. Probably the greatest single threat to any individual, agency, institution, or nation is the loss of proprietary and confidential information. Information security involves protection of all stages of the information cycle. These stages include the creation, use, storage, retrieval, transfer, dissemination, and disposition of information in any form. The level of protection required for each stage in the cycle depends on the value of the information to the organization, the ability of an outsider to duplicate the information, and the potential harm that could result if the information were to be acquired by the wrong individuals, organizations, or nations.

Technical Security

Technical security involves the protection of all electronic systems from loss due to unauthorized access. These systems include, but are not limited to computer, data, and software systems; voice communication; electronic mail; and the Internet.

Operations Security

Operations security involves all measures designed to protect the operation itself. It involves protection of the process through which the operation proceeds. For example, if a critical stage in a manufacturing process were to be lost because of a natural disaster or sabotage, how would this affect the overall operation? Without redundant systems, or backup, even a temporary loss of a critical stage in the operation can result in expensive downtime for the manufacturer.

FUNCTIONS AND RESPONSIBILITIES OF THE SECURITY DIRECTOR

Security management is a multifaceted occupation. As a result, the security director simultaneously assumes managerial, administrative, preventive, and investigative responsibilities. As a *manager*, the security director is responsible for screening, training, scheduling, supervising, and evaluating security personnel. The director also is responsible for safety and security indoctrination and training of all employees. As an *administrator,* the director is responsible for the establishment of the organizational mission, goals, and objectives. This includes planning, financial control, public relations, and community liaison activities.

As the primary *prevention officer* of an agency or business, the security director is ultimately responsible for prevention of loss from any source. It is the responsibility of the director to anticipate, recognize, and appraise risks and initiate action to reduce or remove the risk. As an *investigator,* the director must investigate the potential for loss and the causes of any actual loss that occurs. Auditing or surveying sites, policies, and procedures to ensure that security measures are working is part of the investigative function.

Security management and law enforcement are not synonymous. The language of the security manager is the language of business, not of police work. Similarities between public policing and private security in the actual functions performed often end with the uniformed security officer. Although security personnel may be involved in the detection and investigation of crime and the arrest of suspected criminal offenders, most of their time is spent focusing on preventive efforts to reduce losses from noncriminal sources.

Numerous studies conducted since the 1970s have indicated that former law enforcement officers do not always make good security mangers. In a study conducted by the American Society for Industrial Security, two thirds of the respondents who employed security personnel preferred individuals with specialized training, education, and experience in security services rather than in law enforcement. Business skills, such as planning, accounting, budgeting, public relations, and value-added contribution techniques, are not generally part of police work nor are they the subject of courses taught in police academies. In a 1994 study conducted by the author, consumers of security services, security directors, managers, and security company owners preferred management candidates who possessed skills in general business practices, computer science, accounting, business law, budgeting, contracting, personnel management and labor relations, planning, threat assessment, policy formulation, and statistics. Secondary emphasis was placed on criminal law and investigations.

SECURITY: A GLOBAL PERSPECTIVE

Recent developments in the post–Cold War international arena have given rise to new challenges for security management. Economic competition is replacing political and military power. Industry in the United States is globalizing with American companies conducting business in numerous foreign countries. Competitive pressures are forcing American business to decentralize, search for global markets, create virtual corporations, and become involved in joint ventures. This new way of doing business is creating business vulnerabilities that have not existed before in the history of the world.

Economic security and the protection of proprietary information have become priorities. American businesses are threatened with economic espionage, foreign control, executive kidnapping, terrorism, and narcotics trafficking. Conducting business in foreign countries necessitates special attention to areas not considered when conducting business within U.S. borders. Areas that require special attention include the political climate, currency exchange rates, availability of labor, compliance with local laws and international treaties, cultural and language differences, organized crime, personal and physical security, and disaster preparedness. In 1996, according to the U.S. State Department, there were 109 incidents of political violence against U.S. citizens in foreign countries. Seventy-four of these incidents involved U.S. business executives. American companies must mitigate risks as they conduct business in foreign countries.

ECONOMIC CRIME

Economic crime and industrial espionage probably pose the greatest threats to American business and the security of the United States. Virtually any business and all sorts of information are potential targets. Intellectual property in the form of trade secrets, client lists, financial information, and technical and strategic plans may be of interest to competitors and foreign governments. Information can be stolen electronically through computers or reverse engineering of a product, surveillance, undercover work, hiring an employee away from a company, phony contract negotiations, and bribery. Careful attention must be given to the protection of each stage, or phase, of the information cycle.

RISK ANALYSIS AND THE SECURITY SURVEY

As a method of determining or assessing needs, risk analysis involves a critical, objective, on-site analysis of an organization's entire security system. The processes and instruments used during risk analysis are commonly referred to as *security surveys.* At a minimum, the survey should address the general area or neighborhood surrounding the facility and the perimeter, buildings, restricted areas, organizational policies, safety, personnel and security indoctrination, and education of all employees.

The approach to a security survey may vary. Objective and subjective measures may be used to collect information. Emphasis should be placed on the physical environment, effectiveness of security personnel, policies and procedures, and attitude of management toward the loss prevention function. A more detailed discussion of needs assessment is presented in Chapter 11. A comprehensive survey instrument should be used in the actual on-site survey. Because each type of organization has special needs, it may be necessary to custom design the instrument to be used. Sample surveys are available through a variety of sources, including *The Ultimate Security Survey* (Butterworth-Heinemann, 255 Wildwood Ave., Woburn, MA 01801-2041, 781-904-2500).

CRIME PREVENTION THROUGH ENVIRONMENTAL DESIGN

Overview

Crime prevention through environmental design (CPTED) is based on the theory that the environment can be protected and that crime can be prevented through the proper design of buildings, neighborhoods, and communities. Emphasis is placed on architecture, building codes, and defensible space. It requires that security and safety concepts be incorporated into the planning of a facility or community. In conjunction with community policing programs, CPTED may be applied to residential and business areas to increase public safety and reduce citizen fear of crime.

Security planning through CPTED and the implementation of the recommendations developed as a result of such planning have been effective in preventing and deterring crime. Conversely, poor security planning fails to prevent and deter and encourages crime because the facility or neighborhood design attracts criminal activity. Failure to design residential and business environments with effective safety and security measures may produce a liability connection between victims of crime and property owners, managers, and landlords.

CPTED is not a new concept. In prehistoric times, cave dwellers cleared areas in front of their caves and stacked rocks around the perimeter to mask this space and warn intruders. During the early Greek empire, temple designers used environmental concepts to affect and control behavior. These temples were built of a type of stone that contained phosphorous and reflected a golden light soon after dawn and just before dusk. During medieval times, height was used as defensive tactic. Sleeping quarters were high above ground level and entire communities were walled in. Louis XIV, King of France from 1643 to 1715, was the first to use outdoor lighting on a large scale to reduce crime. Napoleon III (1808 to 1873) authorized his chiefs of police to demolish hideouts for criminals.

CPTED Concepts and Strategies

The conceptual thrust of CPTED is that the environment can be manipulated to produce behavioral effects that reduce the incidence and fear of crime and improve the quality of life. The environment includes people and their physical and social surroundings. Design includes all activities, structures, and policies that seek to positively impact human behavior as people interact with their environment. As such, CPTED focuses on the physical aspects of the environment and on what social scientists, public safety and security personnel, and community organizations can do to safely meet the needs of legitimate users of a space.

CPTED entails traditional target-hardening techniques, such as natural and artificial barrier systems, access control, and surveillance, to reduce the threat from a criminal offender. It also involves strategies developed, implemented, and evaluated by security personnel, law enforcement, and the community to allow for the least restrictive human interface with the barrier systems.

CPTED entails the three-D approach to assessment of human space. The three-D concept is based on three assumptions of how space is to be designed and used (Crowe, 1991). All human space:

1. Has some *designated purpose*
2. Has social, legal, cultural or physical *definitions* that prescribe desired and acceptable behaviors

3. Is *designed* to support and control the desired behaviors

The three basic CPTED concepts of territorial reinforcement, access control, and surveillance are inherent in the three-D approach. These basic concepts may be accomplished through any combination of the following:

1. Provide a clear border definition of the controlled space. Public and private spaces must be clearly delineated.
2. Provide for clearly marked transitional zones. The user must be made to acknowledge movement into the controlled space.
3. Relocate gathering areas. Formally designate gathering areas in locations with good access control and natural surveillance capabilities.
4. Place safe activities in unsafe locations. Safe activities serve as magnets for normal users and communicate to abnormal users that they are at greater risk for detection.
5. Place unsafe activities in safe locations. Vulnerable activities should be placed within tightly controlled areas to help overcome risk and make normal users feel safer.
6. Redesignate the use of space to provide natural barriers. Conflicting activities may be separated by distance and natural terrain to avoid fear-producing conflict.
7. Improve the scheduling of space. The effective use of space reduces risk and the perception of risk for normal users.
8. Redesign space to increase the perception of surveillance. Perception is more powerful than reality.
9. Overcome isolation and distance. Design efficiencies and improved communication systems increase the perception of surveillance and control.

Good planning dictates the tactical implementation of CPTED strategies. Crime analyses, demographic and land use information, and resident or user interviews should be used to plan with CPTED in mind.

Applications of CPTED

CPTED concepts and strategies may be used in a variety of ways. Each situation is unique. No two environmental settings are the same. Some locations where CPTED should be a consideration include the following habitats:

- Commercial facilities
- Streets and highways
- Pedestrian areas
- Parking structures and lots
- Office buildings
- Industrial complexes

- Building hallways and restrooms
- Shopping malls and convenience stores
- Residential areas
- School and college campuses
- Convention centers and stadiums
- Public transit systems

This list is by no means exhaustive. On the contrary, virtually all human functions are amenable to the use of CPTED concepts and strategies. Adaptation to produce a safe and secure environment is unlimited.

SPECIFIC SECURITY APPLICATIONS

Safety and security are a concern in every business or governmental enterprise. The following is a partial list of specific areas in which security management principles are applied:

- Aerospace
- Banking and finance
- Casinos, gaming
- Computer technology
- Construction sites
- Contract services
- Corrections
- Courtrooms
- Education
- Entertainment, sports
- Executive protection
- Government
- Health care
- Hospitality
- Industry
- Insurance
- Investigations
- Law enforcement
- Manufacturing
- Office buildings
- Privatization of public services
- Retail operations
- Residences
- Shopping centers
- Special events
- Strikes, labor disputes

- Utility companies
- Workplace violence prevention

An in-depth discussion of each of these areas is beyond the scope of this book, and although general security principles may apply in each of these settings, each area, and different environments within each area, has unique needs. It is important to remember that security management as an occupational speciality is much more diverse than any other public safety entity.

REFERENCES

Burstein, H. 1996. *Security: A management perspective.* Englewood Cliffs, N.J.: Prentice-Hall.

Crowe, T. D. 1991. *Crime prevention through environmental design.* Boston: Butterworth-Heinemann.

Cunningham, W. C., J. J. Strauchs, and C. J. VanMeter. 1990. *The Hallcrest report II.* Boston.: Butterworth-Heinemann.

Fischer, R. J., and G. Green. 1992. *Introduction to security.* 5th ed. Boston: Butterworth-Heinemann.

Fleissner, D., and F. Heinzelmann. 1996. *Crime prevention through environmental design and community policing.* Washington, D.C.: National Institute of Justice.

Hess, K. M., and H. M. Wrobleski. 1996. *Introduction to security.* 4th ed. Minneapolis: West Publishing.

Jacobson, R. V. 1997. Look through the risk management window to add up security costs. *Access Control and Security Systems Integration* 40 No. 10 (September): 59–62.

Jeffery, C. R. 1972. *Crime prevention through environmental design.* Beverly Hills, Calif.: Sage Publications.

Ortmeier, P. J. 1996. Security education: Adding class to security. *Security Management* 40 No. 7 (July): 99–101.

Schaub, J. L., K. B. Biery, Jr. 1994. *The ultimate security survey.* Woburn, Mass.: Butterworth-Heinemann.

Security Lock Distributors. 1997. *Access control and security systems integration: 1997 salary survey.* Atlanta: Security Lock Distributors.

Chapter 8

Fire Service

HISTORY

Public fire agencies evolved in five basic stages. These stages included the establishment of night fire-watch services; the drafting of fire safety regulations and the appointment of fire protection officers; the organization of groups to salvage building contents from loss due to fire; formation of volunteer fire-fighting agencies; and appointment of paid fire-fighting personnel.

The first organized fire protection probably occurred when Augustus, ruler of Rome in 24 B.C., established a watch service and regulations for preventing fires. One of the earliest recorded fire protection regulations dates back to 872 A.D. in Oxford, England, when a curfew for hearth fires was adopted. Because of the lack of a public fire service, private fire-fighting forces were developed by insurance companies in England in the mid 1600s.

In 1631, a disastrous fire in Boston, Massachusetts, resulted in establishment of the first fire ordinance in the United States. The fire ordinance prohibited thatched roofs and wooden chimneys. In 1648, the first public fire department was established in New Amsterdam. Five men were appointed fire wardens and assumed the responsibilities of fire prevention within the city. In 1679, another huge fire destroyed one hundred fifty-five buildings and several ships in Boston. As a result, more laws were developed, requiring buildings to be constructed of brick or stone and houses to be constructed with slate roofs. The first paid municipal fire department was established in Boston around 1679. By 1715, Boston had six fire companies. Paid municipal fire departments developed slowly in the colonies, however. Most communities used unpaid volunteers or required householders to keep fire buckets and respond to fires in the community when the church bells rang, signaling a fire.

Because of a lack of discipline among most volunteer fire fighters, organized paid fire departments began to replace volunteers in the 1800s. Training also increased. The Boston Fire Department established the first fire school in 1889. New York City established a fire college for advanced officer training, and North Carolina established the first state fire school in 1914. By 1950, most states provided fire service training.

In recent years, the role of the fire service in many communities has expanded far beyond fire suppression. The expanded responsibilities include fire prevention and code enforcement, investigations, community education, incident command, delivery of emergency medical services, environmental safety, and mutual aid. However, fire fighting today is still primarily a local function.

Approximately thirty thousand fire departments exist in the United States. In addition, large industries often provide private fire brigades to protect private industrial complexes. The most common fire service organizations are the public fire department, fire bureaus within a department of public safety, county fire departments, fire districts, fire-protection districts, and volunteer fire companies or associations. Although job titles and duties may differ between fire agencies, the scope of all minimum job requirements are usually those of a paid public fire department fire fighter.

OPERATIONAL UNITS OF A FIRE DEPARTMENT

Regardless of the size of a fire department, it should be organized according to a plan that meets the needs of the community or area it serves. The organizational plan should structure the agency according to the individual functions it is expected to perform. *Line functions* normally are activities related directly to fire suppression and emergency operations. *Staff functions* are nonemergency activities that support line services. Staff functions include fire prevention, training, and fire agency administration.

Fire Suppression and Emergency Operations

Emergency personnel in fire departments are classified as career, on call, or volunteer. The factors influencing the type of personnel used are contingent on the financial resources of the community, the availability of personnel, the frequency of incidents, the range of services expected from the department, and the type of department preferred by the community. Fire fighters within a fire department may be divided into four emergency operational units—engine company, ladder company, rescue company, and special apparatus company.

The fire service relies on four major elements for success—intelligence, personnel, supplies, and good communication. The general public, the business community, and public safety agencies may report fire and other emergencies. It is important that these events be reported effectively. The fire department may receive its communication through public commercial telephone systems, public emergency reporting or fire alarm systems, privately operated automatic alarm systems, or two-way radio communication systems.

Safety is a primary concern for all fire fighters in emergency situations. It is imperative that all equipment and breathing apparatus be routinely maintained. When an emergency situation arises, all fire fighters should wear full protective clothing, use self-contained breathing apparatus, cooperate with their company as assigned, operate tools and equipment carefully, and follow their standard operating procedures (SOP). SOP generally include basic command functions (including a standard method of assuming and continuing command), aspects of communication and dispatching, fireground safety, guidelines that establish tactical priorities, and regular methods of initial resource deployment.

Fire Prevention

According to the National Fire Protection Association, fire prevention is defined as all fire service activity that decreases the incidence of uncontrolled fire. Fire prevention activities include inspections, records and reports, investigations, plan review, hazard abatement, public education, enforcement, company inspection programs, and fire information reporting systems. The responsibilities of fire prevention bureau inspections include the legal means for discovering and correcting deficiencies that pose a fire threat to life and property. The main objective of fire prevention inspections is to ensure that reasonable life safety conditions exist within a given structure. Such inspections are intended to identify hazards that could cause a fire, allow a fire to develop, or allow a fire to spread.

Records and reports involve keeping and maintaining accurate reports of all inspected properties. Accurate records are an essential factor in fire prevention because these inspection files and building reports are necessary for enforcing any fire safety regulations, including those relating to violation notices, plan reviews, and issuance of permits. In addition, well-organized files help to identify occupancies that have automatic sprinklers, standpipe systems, private hydrants, and other private means of fire protection.

Investigation involves determination of the cause of a fire and investigation of criminal actions that may have contributed to a fire. Determination of the cause of a fire is important because analysis of causes and gathered data will indicate trends in certain fire-prone areas. Moreover, the information may lead to a fire prevention program designed to educate the public in specific communities. Investigation of possible arson is also conducted by fire department personnel. Actions taken may vary. In some fire departments, jurisdiction encompasses the arrest and incarceration of arsonists. Other jurisdictions are more limiting, and fire personnel must work with local police authorities in the apprehension of arson suspects.

Plan review involves the role of the fire department in the construction of buildings. This review can be divided into four categories—site plans, preliminary building plans, final building plans and specifications, and certificates of occupancy. The review process is not conducted solely by the fire department. Most sites are reviewed in conjunction with local building, zoning, and public works departments or with authoritative state agencies. Fire officials may participate in preconstruction conferences so they can answer questions relating to building fire-protection features, building codes, fire prevention code requirements, and other plan review processes.

Hazard abatement involves codes for abatement established at the municipal level. Such codes fall within the jurisdiction of fire prevention and focus on building, zoning, planning, electrical, plumbing, heating, air conditioning, forestry, air pollution, and environmental protection. These codes are updated every 5 years and are designed to correlate with the fire prevention standards of the American Insurance Association.

Public education is an important ingredient of fire prevention. The two main purposes of public education are fire prevention education and fire reaction education. Examples of national education campaigns include National Fire Prevention Week in October, Learn Not to Burn, and of course, Smokey the Bear. These campaigns are geared toward community awareness and involvement so that the public is motivated to reduce the risk of fire and take proper action in event of a dangerous fire.

Fire prevention enforcement encompasses adoption of fire prevention codes, code administration, enforcement procedures, and enforcement notices. Enforcement procedures involve the compliance of others with fire permits, certificates, and licenses. Enforcement notices involve fire prevention personnel who inspect occupancies that have been issued warnings or notices of violation, red tag or condemnation notices, citations or summons, or warrants in violation of fire codes. It is the duty of the fire inspector to ensure that corrective action is taken so occupants are in compliance with all fire safety codes.

Company inspection programs include building surveys and correction of common problems concerning life-safety conditions. They also involve locating and correcting fire hazards and testing fire-protection systems. These inspections may be conducted by company personnel, district officers, or by a fire prevention bureau. If hazards are detected and corrective action is warranted, it is the duty of the inspector to conduct all follow-up or repeat inspections.

The National Fire Incident Reporting System (NFIRS) provides the framework for large-scale fire experience databases and reports on almost one-third of all fire incidents. The incident-reporting systems are used to maintain statistics on fires, medical emergencies, and other emergencies to which a fire department responds.

Training

The three main positions in a fire department are fire fighters, fire apparatus driver-operators, and fire fighter emergency medical technicians (EMTs) and fire fighter paramedics. Other supporting fire department positions include motor pump operators, dispatchers, fire alarm dispatchers, automotive mechanics, and fire equipment mechanics. Fire department personnel often supplement fire training agencies with fire science programs offered at community colleges or at universities. In addition, fire service personnel also provide an ongoing forum for special training and the exchange of ideas and information related to fire protection, fire prevention, and fire suppression.

Fire Agency Administration

Administrative activity within a fire department involves budgeting, control, personnel management, and completion of staff reports for the chief of the department. Administrative personnel must have a combination of technical expertise in management and strong negotiation skills, because they often play key roles in obtaining adequate funding and resources for a fire department. Fire department budgets are prepared and submitted by the fire chief to the city or district administration. After the budget receives preliminary administrative approval, it must be approved by the appropriate legislative authority. Once passed, it is effective at the beginning of the fiscal year. To effectively stay within the preset monetary limits, all costs (e.g., personnel staffing, fire apparatus, and vehicles) must be estimated realistically and monitored on a regular basis.

Fire administration personnel are responsible for fiscal management, personnel management, and productivity of operations. In doing so, it is important that each person effectively communicate within and between fire departments to aid in the recruitment, selection, and promotion of personnel to fill the various fire service positions. Fire is a universal threat that affects everyone. Often fire departments affiliate themselves with other departments, agencies, labor organizations, and professional associations. Most affiliates can be linked with the National Fire Protection Association, insurance organizations in the United States with fire protection interests, national fire service organizations, fire research laboratories, and the Society of Fire Protection Engineers. Because fire departments generally are supported by local tax dollars, it is important they maintain and provide good community relations.

A great deal of information regarding fire protection is gathered and classified by fire service agencies. As a result, many fire agencies have revised their data processing to encompass new computer applications. Fire service computer applications may be used for planning, dispatching, incident reporting, inventory of equipment, training purposes, personnel records, code enforcement, and a hazardous materials database. They also are used in the research, management, and engineering departments as aids to new technology.

FIRE PROTECTION SYSTEMS

A fire progresses through four stages. In the *incipient* stage, invisible products of combustion (gases) are released, and no smoke or heat is visible. In the *smoldering* stage, the products of combustion become visible as smoke. In the *flame* stage, an actual fire develops. In the *heat* stage, the temperature increases dramatically, the air expands, and the fire may become uncontrollable.

Fire Sensors and Alarms

Four types of fire sensors are commonly used. They respond to the different stages of fire development. A thermal detector, which provides the least warning time, senses the heat in a protected area. Some thermal detectors are preset and respond at a specific temperature. Others, known as rate-of-rise detectors, respond to rapid increases in temperature. Infrared detectors respond to infrared emissions in flame. Photoelectric detectors, commonly found in residences and many businesses, measure smoke in the environment. Ionization detectors, the most sensitive, respond to invisible products of combustion, such as toxic gases.

Fire alarms fall into two basic categories. Local alarms, or annunciators, sound at the location of the fire. Their purpose is to notify occupants of the residence or facility and summon help from those who are near enough to hear the alarm. Remote signaling systems transmit the fire alarm signal to another location, such as a central station security console, 911 emergency communication center, or fire department.

Fire Extinguishers and Sprinkler Systems

There are five types of portable fire extinguishers. Water fog and foam extinguishers are effective for Class A (ordinary combustibles) and Class B (flammable liquid) fires. Carbon dioxide (CO_2) extinguishers are generally used on Class B and Class C (electrical) fires. Dry-chemical extinguishers are designed to deal effectively with Class A, B, and C fires. Dry-powder extinguishers are effective against Class D (combustible metals) fires. Soda acid extinguishers, which contain water, are used against Class A fires. They are prohibited and no longer manufactured in the United States. Halon gas extinguishers, although expensive, are very effective when used in computer facilities. Production of halon is restricted, however, and the agent may be phased out because it is believed that halon has a negative effect on ozone in the atmosphere.

Sprinkler systems provide one of the best-known protections against personal injury and property loss due to fire. They provide excellent protection in high-rise buildings. These systems use underground or overhead water pipes with sprinkler heads that are plugged with a metal that melts at a specified temperature. Properly installed and maintained sprinkler systems rarely fail to operate if there is an adequate water supply.

PRIVATE FIRE SAFETY EFFORTS

Planning and Training

Life safety and asset protection in the event of a fire depend on good planning and proper training of employees. When a fire occurs or when a fire alarm is sounded, all occupants should react instinctively. All fire alarms should be treated as real. Plans for notification of occupants and fire fighting and other emergency personnel are essential. Evacuation plans and routes must be developed and practiced. Periodic fire-safety inspections are a must.

Educating occupants about fire prevention, fire protection systems, and evacuation procedures is critical to preventing injuries and loss of life. Indoctrination of all new employees and periodic refresher training should be part of every employee's continuing education program. Fire prevention, reporting and evacuation procedures, use of extinguishers, basic first aid, and fire drills should be part of every fire safety training session. Most fires are caused by carelessness, and proper training may help prevent careless acts.

Employee Role in Fire Fighting

In urban settings in which rapid response from a public fire company is almost certain, the need to train business employees to fight fires may be diminished. Some experts might argue that employees should never be asked to participate in fire-fighting activities. After all, life safety is more important than property protection. All fires, no matter how small, require notification of the fire department, and a fire of any magnitude should be left to professionals.

On the other hand, some situations require development of a private company fire unit or fire brigade. Facilities in remote areas away from public fire departments may require an in-house fire-fighting team. Likewise, manufacturing facilities in some foreign countries may not be near adequate fire-fighting services. In these cases, it may be necessary to have a company fire brigade made up of selected, well-trained employees who are competent to handle fire-fighting assignments. The size of a fire brigade depends on the location and size of a facility and on the nature of the fire risk.

REFERENCES

Coleman, R. J. 1990. *Opportunities in fire protection services.* Lincolnwood, Ill.: NTC Publishing.

Fischer, R. J., and G. Green, 1992. *Introduction to security.* Woburn, Mass.: Butterworth-Heinemann.

National Fire Protection Association. 1991. *Fire protection handbook.* 17th ed. Quincy, Mass.: National Fire Protection Association.

Robertson, J. C. 1975. *Introduction to fire prevention.* Beverly Hills, Calif.: Glencoe Press.

U.S. Bureau of the Census. 1996. *Statistical abstract of the United States, 1996.* Washington, D.C.: U.S. Bureau of the Census.

Chapter 9

Environmental Safety

Environmental safety focuses primarily on prevention of harm from hazardous materials. This includes substances that because of certain inherent characteristics are determined by the U.S. Department of Transportation (DOT) to be capable of presenting an unreasonable risk to safety, health, property, and the environment when transported in commerce. Environmental risk is associated with a specific substance, such as asbestos or lead, as the source of the risk. Environmental risk is not simply the absence or presence of a single substance. It involves the source of the risk, the conditions that surround the source of the risk, how a target may become endangered, the extent of the danger, and how it is controlled.

The risk source and the area surrounding that risk source are a whole risk system. An environmental risk should not be viewed as a substance but as a system of components that control the risk. There are four major components of the environmental risk system—risk source, primary control mechanism, transport and secondary control mechanisms, and the target.

The *risk source* is a substance associated with environmental risks. Some risk sources cannot be eliminated, such as radon produced by the natural atomic decomposition of the base rocks of the earth. However, some risk sources can be eliminated. The removal and proper destruction of asbestos is one example. There are advantages and disadvantages to most risk sources. Asbestos, for example, is both a carcinogen and an excellent fire retardant.

The *primary control mechanism* is an agent that controls a risk source. It includes two major components—a physical component in the form of some device that directly maintains the risk source in a benign state and a human component that interacts to guarantee that the physical component performs as it is supposed to. For the risk source to be both useful and benign, both components of the primary control mechanism must be functioning properly.

The *transport and secondary control mechanisms* act as safety nets if any malfunctions occur with the primary control mechanism. There are five transport mechanisms for hazardous materials. They include air movement, direct contact, fire or explosion, ground water, and surface water. Without a transport mechanism, the risk source cannot come into contact with or into the immediate proximity of a target. Therefore it cannot cause any harm to the target. The transport mechanism is associated with several secondary control mechanisms, which may be either artificial or natural in origin. The secondary control mechanisms block transportation and must be evaluated continuously to determine whether harm could occur. Improvement of the risk-to-benefit relationship is the result of development of risk reduction strategies found in the analysis of secondary control mechanisms.

To better understand the transport and secondary control mechanisms, one could use, as an example, the failure of a steel fuel-oil storage tank. The primary control mechanism in this example is the steel storage tank. If it fails, it can release several hundred thousand gallons of fuel oil into a river system. The surface water drainage pattern of the river is the transport mechanism involved in this situation. The secondary control mechanisms are the dike around the fuel-oil tank and the slope of the ground toward the river, which should prevent the fuel oil from reaching the transport mechanism.

Targets include people and sensitive environments. Human targets pose the greatest concern. Considerable resources must be used to analyze the relation between the components of the risk system and to determine the potential effect on targets. The overall analysis of a target is supervised with the negative default principle. This means that the number of possible targets, probable impacts on targets, and failure of primary control mechanisms must be presumed in a worst-case scenario. The mitigating factors are the availability and efficiency of the transport and secondary control mechanisms, the probability of use of the transport mechanism, and the probability of failure of the primary control mechanisms. Examples of targets range from the obvious (human beings, endangered species, and wetlands) to the obscure (designated monuments and environmental areas, such as national parks).

CONCEPTS AND TERMINOLOGY

The concepts and terms associated with environmental safety and the control of hazardous materials include the following:

- Confidence coefficient—a measure of the likelihood that a given answer lies within the confidence interval
- Confidence interval—a measure of the range within which one is likely to find the correct answer
- Dangerous goods—hazardous materials; term used by international regulatory agencies and other sources
- Extremely hazardous substances—chemicals determined by the Environmental Protection Agency (EPA) to be extremely hazardous to a community during an emergency spill or release as the result of their physical or chemical properties or toxicity
- Hazardous chemical—any chemical that presents a physical or health hazard to employees (OSHA)
- Hazardous materials—substances that because of certain inherent characteristics are determined by the U.S. DOT to be capable of presenting an unreasonable risk to safety, health, property, and the environment when transported in commerce

- Hazardous substances—substances identified as hazardous by the EPA under the Clean Water Act and the Comprehensive Environmental Response, Compensation, and Liability Act. The primary thrust of the requirements for transportation of hazardous substances is to communicate the presence of a potential environmental threat and the reportable quantity (RQ) requirements for the substance.
- Hazardous wastes—discarded materials that the EPA regulates under the authority of the Resource Conservation and Recovery Act. In addition to other requirements, hazardous wastes are subject to the Hazardous Waste Manifest Requirements of the EPA.
- Incident—the release or potential release of a hazardous material into the environment (National Fire Protection Association [NFPA])
- Incident commander—the person responsible for all decisions relating to the management of an incident (NFPA)
- Marine pollutant—a hazardous material listed in Appendix B of the U.S. DOT Hazardous Material Table
- Material condition—the physical condition of the primary control mechanism for the material relative to the risk to human health or the environment
- Negative default concept—the concept that for any given environmental risk, one should always assume the worst and attempt to prove that a better situation exists
- Negative leverage—the concept that there is no basis for assuming a relation between the potential cost of an environmental risk liability and the value of a property or operation that may give rise to a liability
- Proof of zero tolerance—the concept that when dealing with risk sources on a property, it is relatively easy to prove that a risk source exists, but it is virtually impossible to prove that one does not exist
- Risk measurement—exposure or opportunity (length of time over which the target is available for contact with the environmental risk) and quantitative impact (kind, type, and severity of the likely results of exposure)
- Transport mechanism—the means by which a risk source can move from its present location to a location where human health may be affected or environmental damage might result
- Zero responsibility—the impossible condition that any party associated in a meaningful way with a property containing a risk source has no responsibility for the possible consequences of the existence of that source
- Zero tolerance—the virtually impossible condition in which no hazardous materials will be permitted on or within a property

IMPACT ON HEALTH

Body Entry Pathways

Hazardous substances may enter the body through any one of four pathways, as follows:

- Absorption. Although the skin acts as a protective barrier for the body, foreign materials may enter if the barrier is weakened. This is especially true if lacerations or abrasions are present. Some solvents also increase the permeability of human skin.
- Ingestion. Toxic substances are swallowed.
- Inhalation. A foreign substance is introduced immediately to the respiratory system and bloodstream. This is the most rapid route of entry.
- Injection. Hazardous substances may be injected accidentally by a bump against, or stepping on, a sharp object.

Toxic Effects

There is a wide range of bodily responses to environmental toxins. The list that follows contains six types of toxic agents, examples of such agents, and the bodily responses they provoke.

- Allergic agents, such as isocyanates, cause itching, sneezing, or rashes.
- Asphyxiants, such as carbon monoxide and hydrogen cyanide, displace oxygen.
- Carcinogens, such as arsenic, asbestos, and cigarette smoke, cause cancer.
- Irritants, such as ammonia, chlorine, and hydrochloric acid, may cause pulmonary edema at very high concentrations or unpleasant sensations throughout the body.
- Necrotic agents, such as nitrogen dioxide and ozone, directly cause cell death.
- Systemic poisons, such as arsenic compounds and benzene, attack the entire body.

Antagonism and synergism are two other concepts related to toxic effects on the human body. An antagonistic effect results when the effect of one agent is decreased by the presence of another agent. Eating bread before drinking alcohol, for example, modifies the immediate effects of the alcohol compared with not eating bread with or before alcohol consumption. Synergism is the enhancing effect of two different environmental contaminants on the human body. Asbestos causes cancer, but the carcinogenic effect of asbestos is two hundred forty times greater for a person who smokes. Similarly, the presence of carbon tetrachloride greatly enhances the narcotic effect of alcohol.

Specific Contaminant Effects

Carcinogens are contaminants that may cause cancer. On average, approximately 15 percent of cases of cancer are related to genetic effects, and 85 percent are related to environmental effects, including both environment and lifestyle. *Mutagens* are agents that cause genetic damage in reproductive cells. Mutagens alter the DNA structure of the genes, and the effects are felt by the next generation.

An example of a mutagen is radiation exposure. *Teratogens* are agents that affect offspring in the fetal stage. Offspring consequently are likely to experience a teratogenic effect because of exposure of the mother to an environmentally hazardous substance. *Latency* is the time period between the exposure of an individual and the clinical manifestation of an adverse effect. An example would be mesothelioma (lung cancer). Workers exposed to airborne asbestos fibers at very high concentrations did not show the effect of cancer until several years after the exposure had ceased.

LAWS

Several laws are devoted to environmental safety. The *Clean Water Act* (CWA) traces its roots to the 1899 Rivers and Harbors Act and the 1972 amendments to the Federal Water Pollution Control Act (FWPCA). The revised FWPCA became the CWA. The CWA regulates the quality of surface water by providing for a permit system that governs the quantity of contaminants that may be discharged into surface waters. National Pollutant Discharge Elimination System (NPDES) permits for a facility determine the kinds and amounts of pollutants that may be discharged by the facility over a certain time period. Section 404 of the CWA provides for dredge and fill permits when the discharge involves a wetland. Dredge and fill permit requirements strictly regulate or may stop any activities in wetlands.

Section 311 of the CWA covers discharges of oil and hazardous substances. The EPA has designated about three hundred substances under Section 311 as hazardous when discharged or spilled. A large number of these substances carry an RQ designation, which specifies the minimum amounts of the substance that must be reported to the National Response Center (NRC) when a spill occurs.

The *Comprehensive Environmental Response, Compensation, and Liability Act* (CERCLA) and its accompanying Superfund were enacted in the late 1980s. This law requires the cleanup of hazardous substances that are released into the environment. CERCLA does not regulate hazardous substances but provides a mechanism for their identification and cleanup. The National Contingency Plan (NCP) established with the CWA was expanded under the CERCLA to include all releases of hazardous substances meeting the RQ designation. NCP established the National Response Team (NRT) and Regional Response Teams (RRTs). Also included in CERCLA are hazardous wastes and regulations promulgated to implement the Resource Conservation and Recovery Act and the hazardous substances identified in Section 311 of the CWA. In 1986, CERCLA was amended with enactment of the Superfund Amendments and Reauthorization Act (SARA).

The *Resource Conservation and Recovery Act* (RCRA) was enacted in 1976 with a major amendment adopted in 1984. The purpose of the RCRA is to promote recycling, control waste disposal, and encourage the use of alternative energy sources. The RCRA established a system to identify wastes and track their disposal, generation, and transportation. The RCRA defines hazardous wastes by listing specific substances considered to be hazardous and defining their characteristics. These characteristics are corrosivity, ignitability, reactivity, and toxicity. RCRA requires that treatment, storage, and disposal facilities (TSDF) have permits to operate. TSDF may be subject to corrective actions designed to reduce environmental risks that have a profound effect on the risk exposure and operations of the facility.

The *Safe Drinking Water Act* (SDWA) protects the drinking water system by setting maximum contaminant levels (MCLs) for public drinking water systems.

The *Clean Air Act* (CAA) regulates both stationary and mobile sources of air pollution and is currently undergoing extensive legislative revision. The CAA governs stationary sources by imposing limitations on emissions.

The *Toxic Substances Control Act* (TSCA) regulates the commercial use, manufacture, and distribution of hazardous chemical products within the United States. The TSCA does not govern the export of hazardous chemical products.

The *Hazardous Materials Transportation Act* (HMTA) regulates hazardous materials transportation, container manufacturers, certain pipelines, commodities not previously defined as hazardous, and routing of hazardous materials.

The *Ports and Waterways Safety Act* (PWSA) protects people, property, and the environment from any harmful effects of hazardous materials and hazardous substances that are transported in large amounts through marine transportation.

The *Sanitary Food Transportation Act* (SFTA) requires that the United States Secretary of Transportation issue regulations to ensure that food and other consumer products are not contaminated during transportation.

The *Hazardous Materials Transportation Uniform Safety Act* (HMTUSA) was signed into law in late 1990. It gave the DOT major new responsibilities in the area of hazardous materials transportation. The HMTUSA extends federal hazardous materials transportation regulations to intrastate transportation and other areas the secretary of transportation deems proper.

The *Occupational Safety and Health Act* (OSHA) is the primary federal law that provides for worker protection from toxic substances. It was established to provide standards of allowable exposure to toxic chemicals in the workplace for persons who could be exposed to a hazardous substance for a period of 40 hours per week. The OSHA standards include setting the permissible exposure limit (PEL), engineering control procedures to mitigate exposure, labeling standards for equipment, standards for personal protection, and monitoring requirements for workers' health.

The *Federal Food, Drug, and Cosmetic Act* (FFDCA) determines the safety of cosmetics, drugs, foods, and medical devices. It bans the intentional addition to food of any substance known to cause cancer in animals (the Delaney Amendment), prohibits pesticide residues on raw agricultural products, and requires a pre-use assessment before Food and Drug Administration (FDA) approval of food additives. The FFDCA, through the FDA, also sets pesticide residue limits for processed foods.

The *Federal Insecticide, Fungicide, and Rodenticide Act* (FIFRA) established a regulatory program, administered by the EPA, to control the manufacture and use of pesticides. It is designed to prevent adverse effects on public health and the environmental risks posed by new pesticides and their persistent characteristics.

PROACTIVE EMERGENCY PLANNING

Business Plans

Businesses that produce, process, transport, and use hazardous materials must establish plans for dealing with these materials. The plans must identify hospitals and other medical resources that have capabilities to provide treatment for injuries resulting from hazardous materials accidents and exposures. The plans must include procedures to reduce the consequences of a release of a hazardous material; that is, a handler must identify actions that will mitigate, prevent, or abate hazards. Procedures must exist to inform employees at a facility and the general public of the presence of a hazardous material. The plans must include programs for initial and refresher training of appropriate employees in (1) the safe handling of hazardous materials used by the business, (2) methods of working with local public emergency response agencies, (3) the use of emergency response resources under control of the handler, and (4) other procedures and resources that will increase public safety and mitigate a release of hazardous materials.

Business plans should analyze the impact of an environmental mishap on the business itself. The cost associated with an environmental disaster can be tremendous. The price tag for preventive measures may pale in comparison to the human and economic costs of deaths, injuries, illnesses, down time, lost revenue, and loss of market, not to mention litigation expenses and adverse lawsuit judgments.

State and Local Plans

State and local area plans also are necessary. Area plans must include provisions for notification of and coordination with appropriate response entities, including those involved with law enforcement, fire suppression, public health, medical response, hospitals, incident control and mitigation, and reception and care of evacuated persons. An area plan must contain provisions to identify and use secondary communication systems such as amateur radio services and cellular or car telephones. Preincident area planning must include clear delineation of the responsibilities of the main response entities for various functions such as site security, fire suppression, and evacuation. Area plans are required to contain provisions for training emergency response employees in ten specific areas, as follows:

1. Emergency procedures. Response personnel must receive training in hazard identification, safe approach to the scene, proper handling of hazardous materials, and a variety of potentially complex incident scenarios.
2. Health and safety procedures. Training must be provided in safe approach, recognition, and evaluation of hazardous materials and proper monitoring and decontamination procedures with training tailored to the hazards present in a particular site.
3. Equipment use and maintenance. Emergency response employees must be trained in the proper use of specialized equipment required to respond to the presence of hazardous materials.
4. Mutual aid. Response organizations must be trained effectively to identify and obtain resources from other jurisdictions.
5. Medical resources. Medical facilities that can properly maintain and administer specific treatment for hazardous materials exposure and contamination must be identified, as should resources outside the area that can provide essential information or treatment.
6. Evacuation. Response personnel must be familiar with specific action protocols such as the distance for security perimeters, evacuation routes, possible release pathways, and reception and care of evacuated persons.
7. Monitoring and decontamination. Emergency response personnel must be trained to recognize, safely remove, and contain hazardous materials.
8. First aid. Emergency response personnel are required to undergo training in basic first aid for injuries from hazardous material accidents to stabilize victims' conditions until a higher level of medical treatment is available.
9. Public information. Training is to be provided in procedures for making necessary safety information available to the public.
10. Psychological stress. Response organizations are required to provide training to reduce the psychological effects of a release of hazardous materials.

EMERGENCY RESPONSE

There are three distinct phases in the emergency response process—the preincident phase, the incident, and the postincident follow-up phase. The *preincident* phase includes hazard communication and product and shipper identification. The critical element of the preincident phase is training of emergency responders at all levels (first responders and others).

The *incident* phase requires information systems and accident notification procedures so appropriate lines of communication can be established to permit effective handling of an incident when it occurs. The emergency response of the parties first at the incident scene, as well as product experts and the detailed follow-up response of emergency response teams, are included in this phase.

The objective of the *postincident* phase is to learn from the experience of handling the incident. To improve the structure of distribution systems, proper feedback and detailed analysis of the incident are necessary. Postincident analysis may reveal both equipment and regulatory shortcomings and when improved design or further legislation and regulation may be warranted.

Elements necessary for an effective emergency response plan include the following:

• Prompt and accurate information about the nature of the incident
• Quick, easy, and accurate identification of the material involved
• Readily available and accurate information concerning product hazard characteristics and measures needed to protect and secure the incident scene
• Ability to dispatch qualified emergency response teams and product specialists to the scene, as required
• Effective lines of communication to involved parties—carrier, shipper, other shippers, emergency response personnel, mutual aid groups, and the news media
• Feedback from the participants' experience with the emergency for use in safety analysis, system improvement, and training

Response actions to an environmental misfortune include the following:

1. Operations and maintenance (O & M) programs designed for long-term maintenance of control mechanisms
2. Repair or restoration of the control mechanism to a functional status
3. Encapsulation—application of an impermeable membrane to prevent the source from gaining access to a transport mechanism
4. Enclosure—construction of an impermeable physical barrier to prevent the source from gaining access to a transport mechanism
5. Isolation—sealing off large areas of risk sources from access to human beings or the environment, possibly permitting access to the source-contained area to trained, equipped, and qualified individuals only
6. Removal and disposal—physical relocation of the source from a high-risk location to a relatively low-risk location or possibly reduction to harmless components or condition

IMPACT ON BUSINESS AND PUBLIC AGENCIES

Businesses and public agencies often have viewed OSHA and the EPA as nuisances that increase the cost of doing business or providing a public service. However, adherence to OSHA and EPA regulations, policies, and procedures can actually strengthen strategies for preventing or reducing losses. Safety consciousness in the workplace did not begin with the passage of OSHA in 1970. The effort to correct unsafe conditions actually began with the passage of the first worker compensation law in Wisconsin in 1911. A growing concern for industrial safety during the twentieth century led the U.S. Congress to apply, through OSHA, a national standard for workplace safety and health. Initial resistance to

OSHA centered on complaints that some of the basic standards went too far or were unnecessary. In recent years, OSHA has made an attempt to promulgate rules that are reasonable and have a direct bearing on workplace health and safety. Today most experts agree that unsafe acts and unsafe conditions are the leading cause of accidents in the workplace. Therefore, regardless of a need to comply with statutorily mandated requirements, common sense dictates a need for a safe and healthy environment.

REFERENCES

Bigelow, C. 1994. *Hazardous materials management in physical distribution.* New York: Van Nostrand Reinhold.

California Occupational Health Program. 1992. *Understanding toxic substances: An introduction to chemical hazards in the workplace.* Sacramento: California Department of Health Services.

California State University. 1994. *Hazardous materials management audit.* San Marcos: California State University.

Fischer, R. 1992. *Introduction to security.* Boston: Butterworth-Heinemann.

Griffin, R. 1988. *Principles of hazardous materials management.* Chelsea, Mich.: Lewis Publishers.

Tyska, L. A., and L. J. Fennelly. 1998. *150 things you should know about security.* Boston: Butterworth-Heinemann.

Wilson, A. 1991. *Environmental risk: Identification and management.* Chelsea, Mich.: Lewis Publishers.

Part Three

The Administrative Process

Chapter 10

Overview of Administrative Process

NATURE OF ADMINISTRATION

Administration may be defined as two or more people who work collaboratively to accomplish a common task or achieve prescribed goals. It emerges from the need for individuals to cooperate with others on complex, difficult, or multiple tasks to achieve common goals of an organization, community, or society. The motivation to cooperate may be based on a reward system that is intrinsic, extrinsic, or both. One might argue that public sector personnel are motivated by intrinsic rewards, such as service, whereas private sector personnel are motivated by extrinsic rewards, such as the potential for high compensation. The author suggests, however, that people may be motivated by various combinations of intrinsic and extrinsic rewards. Public-sector and private-sector employees may ultimately base their motivation to work on how an enterprise is administered.

To understand and appreciate the nature of public safety and security administration, it may be helpful to review the characteristics of public and private administration in general and the principles of organization and management in particular.

With respect to the characteristics of administration, it is helpful to outline the similarities and the differences between public and private administrative practice. The characteristics of public administration include the following:

- Public affairs oriented—focuses on the administration of public agencies and organizations
- Impartial and fair—all citizens are entitled to a particular government service and they must be treated in a uniform manner
- Apolitical—the policies of government may be political, but the detailed execution of these policies is administrative
- Public service oriented—government administration exists to serve the public and profit is not a motive for its operations
- Publicly funded—funds for public administration are appropriated by law and derived from tax revenues

- Publicly documented—administrative records and financial documents are public information that must be made available for review by all citizens
- Accountable to the public—subject to legislative and judicial review at all times
- Selectively staffed (civil service)—qualified personnel are selected on the basis of demonstrated merit through civil service examinations
- Hierarchical—administrative agencies are official and formal and consist of levels of positions

The characteristics of private administration include the following:

- Private enterprise—exists to fulfill a private rather than public obligation or interest
- Private or corporate ownership—owned by a private individual, group, or stockholders
- Competitive—the organization may be in competition with other enterprises engaged in producing the same product or service
- Profit incentive—except for certain nonprofit private organizations, the incentive is to generate net profit
- Financing regulated by market price—revenue based on ability to sell the product or service
- Privacy of information and records (within limits)—information is proprietary and is the property of the owner or owners
- Accountable to owners or stockholders—the organization and its employees are held accountable to the owners rather than the public
- Some freedom in selection and termination—not bound by civil service rules in the hiring or termination of employees
- Freedom in regulating work methods and organization—not bound by civil service regulations

As time passes, the distinction between public and private organizations becomes increasingly blurred. Privatization of public services is but one example. However, similarities and differences continue to exist. Public police and private security officers, for example, have many things in common. They both wear a uniform, compel obedience, prevent and investigate crime, and apprehend suspected criminal offenders. They differ because public police are generally financed through tax dollars whereas private police (security) are financed through profits from businesses. Private security enforces regulations not under the authority of the police. The statutory authority granted to them to arrest, search, and enforce the law are very different in most states.

   In some cases, the characteristics of public and private administration are merged or blended, and a single organization or agency may assume the characteristics of both private and public organizations. Examples include some nonprofit organizations and quasigovernmental institutions. Regardless of the nature of the institution, public or private, the administrative process focuses on generic principles of organization and management. *Organization* generally refers to the structural component of administration; *management* focuses on the fluid and dynamic process of administration.

From a structural standpoint, the traditional principles of organization include the following:

- Similar tasks are grouped together
- Specialized units or departments are formed when necessary
- Lines of demarcation between responsibilities are clearly established
- Communication channels are established
- Structure and common terminology are used
- Unity of command is developed—one person, one boss
- Span of control is exercised—appropriate for effective supervision
- Each task is assigned to someone (responsibility)
- Supervision for each person is required of someone
- Authority is commensurate with responsibility
- Persons are accountable for tasks

The level of complexity within an organization depends on the amount of horizontal and vertical differentiation that exists. Horizontal differentiation is usually based on activity. This activity may be associated with the type of clientele, style of service, geography, time, or process. Vertical differentiation is based on levels of authority.

Complexity within an organization is not always based on size. Small departments, agencies, or businesses may be very complex in organizational design. Some organizations have narrow spans of management control with tall structures and many levels. Other organizations increase the span of control and shorten the organizational structure, reducing levels of management. There is no one-size-fits-all structure, and there are advantages and disadvantages associated with each design. Tall organizations with narrow spans of control, for example, place fewer demands on supervisors while increasing problems with communication and vice versa.

Organizations may be differentiated on the basis of line, staff, function, or project orientation. *Line* refers to elements that perform the tasks for which the organization was created. *Staff* refers to elements that support the line, such as communication and laboratory facilities. *Functional* structures, although complex, improve communication between elements because delegation of management authority extends beyond normal spans of control. Intelligence activities in a police department, for example, may cross all lines of authority. The essence of the *project* structure is that elements from various segments of the organization may be assigned to task forces to work on specific problems or situations.

The structural component of an institution is often represented in the form of an organizational chart. In the latter half of the twentieth century, however, the introduction of computer power changed the way in which many institutions operate. Many institutions moved away from the hierarchical or military structural model to a flatter, more collegial organization built around shared information. As a result, middle management, which in the past functioned as the conduit between chief executive officers and line personnel, has been eliminated. The organizational structure becomes decentralized. Each member of the organization becomes the member of a team that is innovative, participatory, flexible, and adaptable. The resurrection of team policing and its transformation to community policing illustrates this trend. In a community policing environment, for example, the line police officer operates with less direct supervision and is much more directly involved with assisting the community client in the identification and development of solutions to community problems.

The fluid and dynamic process of administration focuses on the principles of management. The traditional principles of management include the following:

- Planning
- Organizing
- Staffing
- Directing (or leading)
- Controlling (or evaluation)

Planning involves thinking ahead by selecting future courses of action based on an identified need. Organizing involves the collection and development of physical, financial, and human resources necessary to achieve the goals articulated in the planning process. Staffing is the process of hiring, training, and rewarding people for doing the work of the organization. Directing, or leading, involves guiding people to achieve the goals of the organization. Controlling, or evaluation, involves comparing actual performance with planned performance.

COMMON PRINCIPLES IN ADMINISTRATION

Whether an organization conforms to traditional or modern principles of organization and management, common elements exist in all administrative processes. If one were to blend the ingredients of organization and management into one format, the common elements of the single format would include the following areas.

Planning

- Assess the need
- Develop alternative courses of action
- Select an action plan

Implementation (Putting the Plan into Operation)

- Organize
- Staff (human resource management)
- Acquire equipment and facilities
- Develop policy statements
- Allocate and deploy resources

Leadership and Ethics

- Lead and maintain an ethical standard

Evaluation

- Monitor progress
- Control and follow up

These common elements to administration are explored in more depth in Chapters 11 through 14.

ISSUES FACING MODERN ADMINISTRATION

Organizational Cultures and Subcultures

People in an organization often share common beliefs and behavior patterns. Organizational culture, therefore, is a pattern of shared meaning. It is this pattern of shared meaning, mission, and purpose of which administrators must have intimate knowledge to function effectively.

Hofstede, Neuijeu, Ohayv, and Sanders (1990) outlined the dimensions of organizational culture. These dimensions include the following:

- Member identity—the degree to which individuals identify with the organization as a whole rather than with some subgroup or specialization
- Group emphasis—the degree to which work is organized around groups rather than individuals
- People focus—the extent to which management considers the effects of its decisions on people in the organization
- Unit integration—the amount of encouragement of coordinated, interdependent activity among units
- Control—the degree to which rules and supervision are used to control employees

- Risk tolerance—the encouragement of risk and innovation
- Reward criteria—the extent to which rewards are based on performance rather than seniority or favoritism
- Conflict tolerance—the degree to which the open airing of conflict is encouraged
- Means-end orientation—the extent of managerial focus on outcomes and results rather than processes
- Open-system focus—the amount of monitoring of external developments

Subcultures may develop within an organization around specialized work-groups and units. Likewise, the organization is influenced by cultures external to the organization, such as communities, competition, political action groups, citizens, and customers. Regardless of any experience, education, or training, an individual tends to adopt attitudes and blend into the culture of a group or organization.

Organizational Learning

Organizations today face continuous and rapid change. It is no wonder, then, that organizations also face the need for continuous learning. Organizations must do more than simply encourage members to learn. They must establish the mechanisms for system-level learning. To be successful, all members, units, and departments of an organization must be involved in the organizational learning process.

The four-step model that represents the system-level learning process includes the following: (1) Information is generated as individuals in the organization interact with the external environment or experiment to create new information internally. (2) The new information is integrated into the organization. (3) All available information related to an issue is collectively interpreted. (4) Action is taken on the basis of interpretation. The action generates feedback, and that new information helps to return the members to the first step to begin the cycle again. Information, which is gathered internally and externally, processed, and shared with the members of the organization, can assist the organization in the discovery of new problems, solutions, and opportunities.

Performance in Organizations

High performance is usually found in a learning organization that has a focused mission and a community culture. In such an organization, leaders understand that their key role is to provide conditions that enable employee productivity. High performance organizations can be identified when the following happen:

- Anyone in the organization can articulate its mission and values.
- The organization is always looking into something new.
- Customer satisfaction level is high.
- A failure is considered a learning experience.
- Employees frequently work in teams.
- The leader is a partner to the staff members.
- Others study and write about the organization, and everyone wants to take credit for its accomplishments.
- The organization can give relevant information on its program results.
- The organization is a laboratory and its own best model.

In summary, productivity and performance are high in an organization that has a clearly defined and articulated mission; focuses on the consumer, client, customer; provides employees with avenues for input on decision making; and fully involves employees in managing their work.

REFERENCES

Dixon, N. 1995. *A practical model for organizational learning: Issues and observations.* Greensboro, N.C.: Center for Creative Leadership.

Hale, S. J. 1996. Achieving high performance in public organizations. In *Handbook of public administration*, edited by J. L. Perry. San Francisco: Jossey-Bass.

Hofstede, G., B. Neuijeu, D. D. Ohayv, and G. Sanders. 1990. Measuring organizational cultures: A qualitative and quantitative study across twenty cases. *Administrative Science Quarterly* 35, 286–316.

Mosley, D. C., L. C. Megginson, and P. C. Pietri, Jr. 1993. *Supervisory management: The art of empowering and developing people.* Cincinnati: South-Western Publishing.

Peak, K. J. 1995. *Justice administration: Police, courts, and corrections management.* Upper Saddle River, N.J.: Prentice-Hall.

Perry, J. L., ed. 1996. *Handbook of public administration.* San Francisco: Jossey-Bass.

Souryal, S. S. 1981. *Police organization and administration.* San Diego: Harcourt Brace Jovanovich.

Swanson, C. R., L. Territo, and R. W. Taylor. 1998. *Police administration: Structures, processes, and behavior.* 4th ed. Upper Saddle River, N.J.: Prentice-Hall.

Trice, H. M., and J. M. Beyer. 1993. *The cultures of work organizations.* Englewood Cliffs, N.J.: Prentice-Hall.

Chapter 11

Planning

The need for proper planning cannot be overemphasized. Planning is probably the most crucial factor in the success of every organization. Planning includes an analysis of the current situation, a forecast of future events, the establishment of objectives, priorities, and a decision about which course of action will most appropriately achieve the objectives. To be effective, planning must precede all other management and administrative functions. Thorough planning results in better resource utilization. It promotes efficiency, reduces costs, and eliminates waste.

TYPES OF PLANS

There are several types of plans. Some are single-use and others are repeat-use. Other types include tactical, strategic, and contingency plans. Single-use plans are no longer needed once the objectives of the plan are met. Budgets and special projects are examples of single-use plans. Repeat-use (standing) plans may be used again and again. They are followed each time a given situation or incident occurs. Unless modified, repeat-use plans change little over time. Examples of repeat-use plans include policies, procedures, and methods for achieving objectives. Tactical plans are short range and are scheduled to be executed within a short period of time. Strategic plans, on the other hand, are long range and may involve plans that are scheduled to be implemented over a period of years. Contingency plans are those implemented only if certain events, such as natural disasters or emergencies, occur.

There may be several versions of each type of plan. Contingency planning, for example, requires a different plan for each kind of emergency. Some plans are simple, and others are complex. The response to an accident requiring basic first aid may be relatively simple, but a response to a natural disaster may be very detailed and complex. Natural disasters may affect an entire community or region. The following outline illustrates the detail and comprehensiveness associated with a major disaster plan:

1. Authority—from chief executive officer to designated emergency coordinator

2. Purpose—clearly stated transition from normal to emergency operation
3. Types of emergencies covered
4. Execution instructions
5. Supporting information
    * Maps
    * Procedure charts
    * Telephone lists
    * Local resource list
    * Mutual-aid agreements
    * Liaison with Federal Emergency Management Agency (FEMA)
    * Glossary
6. Emergency Control Center, Emergency Operations Center
    * Location
    * Communication
    * In-house communication
7. Protection of vital records
    * Agency records
    * Data files
    * Incorporation certificate
    * Client lists
    * Bylaws
    * Stock records
    * Board meeting minutes
    * Financial records
8. Emergency shutdown procedures
9. Protection of personnel
10. Evacuation and movement to shelter
11. Education and training, emergency plan manual
12. Testing the plan
13. Role of supervisors

TRADITIONAL STEPS TO PLANNING

Traditional planning processes contain up to nine steps. These traditional steps in the planning process may include the following:

* Recognize the need for a plan
* Formulate a statement of objectives
* Collect and analyze relevant data
* Develop details of the plan
* Obtain agreement from the operational units that will eventually carry out the plan (Wilson 1952)

COMMON ELEMENTS IN PLANNING

Regardless of the number of steps involved in a single planning process, common elements exist in all planning. These include a needs assessment, development of alternative courses of action, and selection of an action plan.

Needs Assessment

The first step is to establish the need or frame of reference for a plan. It must be determined whether an actual need exists or a perceived need is simply based on desires or special interests. It is also necessary to collect and analyze relevant data. This data may be collected by means of both subjective and objective measurements. *Subjective measures* include the use of forecasting, expert opinion, and the Delphi technique. The Delphi technique involves a process whereby several individuals or experts provide input on a given issue and ultimately arrive at consensus on a prediction or list of needs and priorities. *Objective measures* may include the following:

- Audits
- Marketing
- Operations research
- Statistical reports
- Threat assessment
- Investigations
- Risk analysis
- Inspections
- Surveys

For example, a survey may be used for safety and security planning. It involves a critical, objective, on-site analysis of an organization's entire security system. The survey instrument used should address, at a minimum, the following areas:

- The *general area or neighborhood* surrounding the facility with consideration of area crime rates, aesthetic qualities, and susceptibility to catastrophic events such as floods
- The *perimeter* near the facility in terms of its parking, fencing, landscaping, and signs
- The *buildings* themselves, including points of entry, exits, access control, locks and keys, alarm systems and lighting, and vulnerability to intrusion
- *Restricted areas* within the facility, including computer and data storage areas, key storage areas, mechanical and utility rooms, telecommunication rooms, mailrooms, and executive office suites

- *Organizational policies*, including an analysis of procedures used in the management of human resources and the protection of property and information
- *Safety procedures*, including mechanisms for prevention of accidents as well as fire safety and emergency plans for disasters
- *Number of security personnel* required and personnel responsibilities and training requirements
- *Indoctrination and education* of all employees regarding security and safety policies and procedures

Develop Alternative Courses of Action

Once the needs (goals) are identified, objectives for meeting the needs are outlined. This involves development of action plans that include measurable objectives. Decisions with respect to courses of action and selection of the most appropriate action plan have to be made. Each alternative must be evaluated to determine probable undesirable and desirable consequences. This involves conscious consideration and selection of a course of action from among available alternatives to produce the best possible result.

Some types of decisions are programmed, that is, they are routine and repetitive and handled systematically, such as work schedules. Other decisions are not programmed. Rather, they are infrequent, such as which contingency plan to implement in the event of a natural disaster. The decision-making process and the decisions made may not always be popular. The impact of the decision on the organization, its people, its clients, and the community also requires careful consideration. Decisions may cause stress and anxiety. However, if well thought out, each decision may be viewed as an opportunity for development, progress, and advancement of individual and organizational goals and objectives.

The financial effect of each action plan must be determined. This requires a budget for each plan. Although viewed by some as a laborious task, budget preparation should be viewed as an integral part of the planning process. It is an essential planning tool and should be tied to the established goals and objectives developed as alternative courses of action. The budget is a comprehensive plan expressed in financial terms. Areas to consider in budget preparation include past operations, present conditions, and future expectations. Revenue forecasts, client population demands, and projected expenditures to meet the demand all are part of budget preparation. The budget process should be continuous, flexible, and responsive to the changing needs of the organization. There are several types of budgets, including the following:

- Traditional—simple percentage increase over past budget
- Line item—description of item and the cost of each item. The advantages of line-item budgets are that they provide detail, clarity, and are easy to audit. The disadvantages include inflexibility and isolation from the objectives.

- Performance based—includes measurable units tied to the objectives and allows for a cost-benefit analysis according to program type. The disadvantage to this type of budget is that some items are not easily measured, e.g., the number of crimes or accidents prevented as a result of money spent on a security system.
- Zero-based budgeting (ZBB)—each program in each budget period must justify its existence and expenditures

Regardless of the type of budget used, the elements of a budget should include provision for personnel, operating expenses, supplies and materials, capital expenditures, and miscellaneous expenditures. The elements of a budget are as follows:

1. Personnel
   - What type and how many? List salary (weekly, bi-weekly, twice each month, monthly) or wages (hourly).
   - Mandated personnel-related expenses. Federal Insurance Contributions Act (FICA), otherwise known as Social Security. Assume 7.5 percent (0.075) of first $65,400 salary and wages for each employee, maximum of $4,905.00.
   - Medicare. Assume 1.45 percent (0.0145) of all salary and wages for each employee.
   - Federal Unemployment Insurance (FUTA). Employees pay no part of this tax. Assume 6.2 percent (0.062) of each employee's salary and wages up to $7000 per year ($56.00 maximum).
   - State Unemployment Insurance (SUTA). Federal rate for FUTA may be reduced by an amount equal to the state rate. Assume 0.3 percent to 5.4 percent (depending on employer's rate) of first $7,000.
   - Employment Training Fund (ETT). Assume 1 percent of first $7,000 of salary and wages up to $7,000 per year.
   - State Disability Insurance, California (SDI). Although the employer deducts this from employees' pay, the employer is not responsible for this tax. Therefore it is not an expense item for the employer.
   - Discretionary personnel–related expenses. Health insurance, retirement, vacations, sick leave.
   - Overtime pay for hourly employees. Salaried employees are generally exempt.
2. Operating Expenses
   - Rent
   - Utilities
   - Contracted services
   - Training (before service and in service, career enhancement)
   - Telephone (local and long distance)
   - Insurance (liability, accident, flood, earthquake, fidelity)
   - Professional fees (attorney, consulting, accounting)

- Pre-employment screening (drug testing, background investigations)
- Taxes (vehicle, unless exempt)
- Advertising expense (e.g., help-wanted ads)
- Memberships in professional organizations
- Computer database services (Internet access subscription, criminal and credit history checks)

3. Supplies and materials (objects with an expected life of 1 year or less)
   - Office supplies
   - Software
   - Ammunition
   - Fuel

4. Capital expenditures—depreciable assets or objects with an expected life of 1 year or more. Large capital expenditures may require a separate capital budget. These expenditures may be amortized over a period of years.
   - Equipment
   - Buildings
   - Computers
   - Pagers
   - Autos (Note: White autos have a greater resale value, up to $800 in 1996)
   - Firearms

5. Miscellaneous
   - Travel
   - Entertainment
   - Depreciation (of capital assets)

Selection of Action Plan

To select the most appropriate action plan, the participants in the budget process must analyze the capabilities of the organization. In other words, a determination of available resources must be made. Financing (funding) for public organizations may be generated through taxes, donations, grants, contracts, bonds, enforcement revenue, and fees. Private organizations may be financed through sales, grants (there are more than twenty-six thousand private foundations in the United States), and contracts. In some cases, resources may be shared with other businesses, organizations, and agencies through the use of consortia and articulation agreements. For example, a California State Public Safety Training Consortium was developed in 1994 among police, fire, corrections, hazardous materials, and private security agencies to share training resources. In other cases, the department or agency may generate revenue by selling service to another organization. For example, the cost of establishing and maintaining a central station alarm system may be offset through a contractual arrangement to monitor another business's alarms.

Support must be generated for the action plan recommended. The types of support needed for effective implementation include the following:

• Organizational. Positive employee relations require that employees be involved in the decision-making process or at the very minimum be informed as to the nature of, and reason for, future plans. People tend to experience difficulty with change, whether that change is negative or positive.

• Community. When the community is to be affected by the implementation of the plan, information should be disseminated on a need to know basis to generate public support. This may be accomplished through the news media, public-speaking engagements in community forums, and at meetings of professional organizations. Examples of planned activities where community involvement is critical may include a new enforcement strategy for a police department or construction of a theme park by a private company or developer.

• Consumer. Who are the consumers of the action plan? Are they employees, the public, or individual customers? Regardless of who the consumers are, it is important that those who might be considered clients of the plan be informed as to its nature, scope, and intent.

• Entity responsible for approval of the budget. Who is responsible for approving the budget? Is it management, the legislature, the city council, a department head, a foundation, or a granting agency? A strategy must be developed to justify the budget to all the principal stakeholders. It, or they, will want to know what value the plan, if implemented, will contribute to the goals and objectives of the organization or agency.

• Other organizations. If the plan involves other organizations and agencies, liaison should be established with them. For example, a law enforcement agency may require assistance from other jurisdictions to implement the plan. Likewise, corporate security departments tend to be more effective when liaison is established with relevant public safety agencies. Similarly, if resources are to be shared through a consortium, planning must involve the other organizations affected by the plan. Liaison with other agencies may be a necessity. For example, given the reality that the crime rate, although declining in recent years, remains relatively high, cooperation between law enforcement and private security is essential. Strong alliances have been developed between the public and private sectors in many areas of the United States. Public-private partnerships, such as the Virginia Police and Private Security Alliance and the East Bay Public Safety Corridor Partnership in San Francisco, and the use of private security on public transit systems are but a few examples of how cooperation and complementary relationships can benefit all citizens.

REFERENCES

Barefoot, J. K., and D. A. Maxwell. 1987. *Corporate security administration and management.* Boston: Butterworth-Heinemann.

Bentley, S. W. 1997. An alliance is born. *Security Management* 40 No. 10 (October): 77, 78, 80.

Bureau of Justice Assistance. 1997. *East Bay public safety corridor partnership.* Washington, D.C.: U.S. Department of Justice, Office of Justice Programs.

Drucker, P. 1974. *The practice of management.* New York: Harper & Row.

Kenney, J. 1959. *Police management planning.* Springfield, Ill.: Charles C Thomas.

Moses-Schulz, D. 1997. Private security comes on board. *Security Management* 41 No. 4 (April): 59, 60, 62, 63, 65.

Mosley, D. C., L. C. Megginson, and P. H. Pietri. 1993. *Supervisory management: The art of empowering and developing people.* Cincinnati: South-Western.

Perry, J. L., ed. 1996. *Handbook of public administration.* San Francisco: Jossey-Bass.

Price, J. E., M. D. Haddock, and H. R. Brock. 1996. *College accounting.* 8th ed. New York: McGraw-Hill.

Souryal, S. 1981. *Police organization and administration.* New York: Harcourt Brace Jovanovich.

Wilson, O. W. 1952. *Police planning.* Springfield, Ill.: Charles C Thomas.

Chapter 12

Implementing the Plan

ORGANIZATION

The first step in the implementation of the action plan selected is to organize the operation. Traditional principles of organization are discussed in Chapter 10. Traditional organizations, large or small, tend to share the following basic principles:

- A set of goals and objectives
- A method of grouping the activities performed by the organization
- Segregation of line, staff, and auxiliary functions
- Specialization of tasks or personnel
- A hierarchy of authority
- A span of control that determines the number of subordinates under the control of a superior
- Delegation of authority
- Unity of command that provides each employee with only one "boss"
- A system of formal communication

As discussed in Chapter 10, many organizational structures in the latter half of the twentieth century became more collegial. As a result, middle management was reduced, and subordinates and supervisors functioned more as colleagues. Whether based on traditional or collegial principles, the organizational structure or framework of a business or governmental agency varies depending on size, location, budget, and methods of operation. Organizational structures typically are presented in the form of organizational charts.

HUMAN RESOURCE MANAGEMENT

The second major step in implementation of a plan is to staff the department, agency, or business. Regardless of the type of organization, basic elements exist in the management of human resources. These elements are included in the process of determining how many people the organization needs, what they will do, and how they will be hired, trained, led, and evaluated. Areas to consider when staffing any organization include the following.

Staffing Requirements

The first step in human resource management is to determine how many people are needed. For example, if a person is to be assigned to a workstation or post 24 hours a day, 7 days a week, the equivalent of 168 clock hours, it is estimated that 4.5 full-time equivalent (FTE) persons will be needed to cover this assignment. This takes into account vacations and sick leave without unnecessary overtime. This position can be filled with any combination of full or part-time employees.

Occupational (Job Task) Analysis

Once the number and types of persons or employees needed are determined, it is necessary to conduct an analysis of the tasks the person in this position is expected to perform. This analysis can be accomplished through direct observation or by means of comparing this position with similar positions in or outside the organization. The tasks may be identified by means of interviewing current employees, managers, and other employers.

The first step in job task analysis is to identify the job functions (duties) a worker is expected to perform. Once the job functions have been identified, desired job behaviors are analyzed to determine future training needs. Finally, each behavior must be analyzed in terms of the actual performance of the behavior, in other words, how the worker's behaviors are to be measured.

Job Description

A job description, often referred to as a position description, is a written description of the principal duties of the job. It identifies the principal elements, scope of authority, and responsibilities involved in the job. Tabulating the results of the task analysis and reviewing the results with appropriate staff assist in this process. The job description should be reviewed and revised annually.

Job Specifications

Closely aligned with the occupational analysis and job description are the job specifications. Whereas the job description describes the main duties of a position, the job specifications outline the specific skills, competencies, and personal qualifications necessary to perform the job adequately. The job description and job specifications may appear in the same document.

Recruitment

Recruiting candidates to fill a position vacancy may be accomplished in a variety of ways. It may be accomplished internally through promotion, transfer, or upgrading the position itself. External recruiting may take place through the use of the following sources:

- Newspapers and periodicals
- Colleges and universities
- The Internet
- Former employees
- Friends and relatives of employees
- Personal applications on file
- Labor organizations
- Employment agencies
- Job fairs

Instruments used as employment applications should be objective, uniform, consistent, and job-task related. Caution should be exercised in the development of application forms to ensure that information is not requested in violation of any state or federal statute. Items that might create an illegal or potentially illegal inquiry include address, age, birthplace, race, citizenship, religious affiliation, and arrest or conviction information. Public organizations, however, such as law enforcement agencies may request information that a private organization may not. For example, as a rule, private organizations have access to conviction data but not arrest records, because conviction records are public information.

Selection

The selection process begins with a preliminary screening of applicants. This involves a review of each application packet to ensure that the candidate meets the qualifications and specifications for the position. The preliminary screening may involve pre-employment aptitude tests, physical agility tests, medical examinations, criminal history and credit checks, and a polygraph examination (public sector only). Employers must exercise a great deal of care in the pre-employment screening process. Failure to exercise due diligence in the pre-employment process may establish a liability connection with the candidate or the candidate's behavior if the candidate becomes an employee. The last phase of the selection process involves interviewing and checking of references. Care should be exercised to avoid questions that may be in violation of local, state, and federal statutes relative to equal employment opportunity.

Training

Employee training falls into three broad categories—preservice, in service, and career enhancement. With respect to preservice training, some occupational specialities have prescribed training before employment. For example, public safety employees, such as those in police, fire, and corrections agencies, have specific detailed preservice training requirements. In-service training may be formal or informal. It may involve apprenticeships, internships, or on-the-job training. Career enhancement includes educational experiences that focus not only on specific job-related training but also on experiences that promote the personal and professional development of the individual. Substantial returns on the training investment may be realized if the organization focuses on individual career enhancement. Benefits in terms of increased productivity, improved morale, and loyalty to the organization are the positive by-products of an individualized career-enhancement program.

Scheduling

Employees should be scheduled according to a plan based on need and productivity requirements. Employee work schedules are generally based on the assumption that individuals are willing to work at 100 percent capacity. Supervisors should realize, however, that not all employees can be expected to work continuously at top speed. Therefore adequate personnel have to be assigned to a set of tasks to ensure that personal productivity needs are met. Caution should be exercised to account for absences and reduce the need for overtime. Nontraditional scheduling arrangements and part-time or contract employment may be used as alternatives to full-time regular employment. Employees are the most important resource of an enterprise. If the organization is thorough in its pre-employment screening process, hires the right people, maintains their integrity, and promotes their individual personal and professional well-being, most, if not all, employees in the work force will perform well and as close to 100 percent capacity as is humanly possible.

Supervision and Leadership

Supervision, or the management of human resources, should not be confused with leadership. Leadership, a concept broader than management, occurs any time one attempts to motivate, influence, or mobilize any individual or group. (The concepts of leadership and ethics are addressed in more detail in Chapter 13.) In the management of human resources, the focus is on supervision, which involves directing people toward organizational goals. Managers and supervisors therefore bring a measure of order and consistency to organizations by planning, budgeting, organizing, staffing, and controlling. Not all supervisors make good leaders and vice versa.

Performance Appraisal

A performance appraisal involves the systematic assessment of how well employees are performing. A performance appraisal should focus on performance, not the person, on strengths as well as weaknesses, and should be designed to enhance performance. The ideal appraisal or evaluation process includes, at a minimum, the supervisor's evaluation of the employee and a self-evaluation made by the employee. In addition, some formal appraisal processes include peer evaluations and evaluations of the employees by clients or consumers of the employee services.

The appraisal meeting itself is the most important part of the appraisal process. It should be constructive, emphasize strengths, and point out areas for improvement and the means for achieving future goals. Appraisal meetings should be held in private with adequate, uninterrupted time allotted for open, honest, and frank discussion. The content of the appraisal meeting should be kept strictly confidential, because the discussion may often include expressions of opinion and criticism.

Promotion

Promotion should serve as an incentive for employees to perform better. Employees with the best records with respect to production, quality of work, and cooperation should be the ones promoted. However, because of financial constraints, or inability to measure performance objectively, salary increases and promotions may be difficult. Virtually all employees expect to be rewarded for a job well done. Promotion or assistance with professional development is extremely important. If promotion from within is difficult, even though a promotion is warranted, a progressive manager may choose to assist the employee with a transfer or new job search. If promotion from within is possible, it may be accomplished through mechanisms such as seniority, merit, or ability to perform specific tasks.

Not all employees wish to be promoted. Some, although excellent employees, may choose to remain in their current position. Others may not function well in the position to which they would be promoted. For those who are good candidates and seek promotion, the competition for promotion may be intense. The promotion process should be fair, objective, and based on the candidate's ability to perform in the new position. The competitive process should involve use of standardized, objective assessments of the candidate's qualifications and current performance and an evaluation of the candidate's strengths and weaknesses as a prediction of future performance.

Discipline

The purpose of disciplinary action should be to improve performance and behavior rather than to punish or seek revenge. Discipline is related to the word *disciple*, which means "follower." *Follower* is derived from the Latin word *discere*, which means "to learn." Therefore the disciplinary process should serve to educate the employee. Except in rare instances in which immediate termination may be warranted by policy or law, a system of uniformly applied progressive discipline may be used. With this system, corrective action progresses through the following steps: verbal warning, verbal warning noted in employee's record, written reprimand, suspension or demotion, and termination.

The agency or business should establish a written policy that addresses uniform standards of behavior. These standards may include the following:

1. Habitual tardiness and absenteeism
2. Actual or attempted theft of company or agency property
3. Fighting or bodily injury to others
4. Malicious mischief or harassment
5. Intoxication on duty
6. Possession of illegal drugs or alcohol on duty
7. Refusal or failure to comply with supervisory instructions
8. Inattention to duties (sleeping, idleness)
9. Violation of published safety or health rules
10. Unauthorized possession of weapons or explosives
11. Sexual harassment of anyone while on duty

If disciplinary action is warranted, it must be based on an objective standard. Questions that should be answered before any such action include the following:

1. Were employees forewarned concerning consequences?
2. Was the task or rule reasonable?
3. Did the firm or agency verify the violation before taking disciplinary action?
4. Was the investigation thorough and fair?
5. Was there substantial evidence of guilt?
6. Were rules and penalties enforced uniformly?
7. Was the disciplinary action appropriate to the situation?

SPECIAL ISSUES IN HUMAN RESOURCE MANAGEMENT

Chemical Abuse and Drug Testing

All organizations should have written policies with respect to chemical abuse on duty and in the workplace. These policies must be communicated to each employee. Care should be exercised to ensure that chemical abuse policies and disciplinary procedures derived therefrom are consistent with applicable laws. Drug testing in the workplace is an extremely sensitive issue. Although government regulations may require drug testing in certain types of occupations, case law with respect to the constitutionality of drug testing in the workplace generally is inconclusive.

Complaints and Grievances

A clearly defined policy and procedure should be developed to address employee complaints and grievances. Usually these procedures progress from the informal to the formal stages. In a nonunion organization, the procedure begins with the immediate supervisor and progresses through middle management to the chief executive officer and, possibly, an outside arbitrator. In a union organization, this process occurs in liaison with union representatives. Essentially this means that the complaint or grievance is filed by the employee with the union steward and progresses through a union committee and the union president toward outside arbitration if warranted and necessary.

Sexual Harassment

Sexual harassment may be defined as any unwelcomed sexual advances, requests, or conduct. A growing number of court cases address the problems of sexual harassment. These court cases and decisions have generally held that an employer is liable if sexual harassment is in any way condoned or improperly investigated and if corrective action is not taken. All organizations should have a clear, written, no-harassment policy.

LEGISLATION IMPACTING EMPLOYER-EMPLOYEE RELATIONS

Organizations must address the following legislative mandates:

- *Title VII of the Civil Rights Act*—prohibits employment decisions based on race, color, religion, sex, and national origin
- *Executive Order 11246 of the Civil Rights Act*—added on the requirement of affirmative action to Title VII
- *Age Discrimination in Employment Act*—prohibits employment decisions based on age when person is 40 years of age or older.
- *Pregnancy Discrimination Act*—prohibits employers from discriminating against pregnant women
- *Worker Adjustment and Retraining Act*—requires employers to notify workers of impending layoffs

- *Drug-free Workplace Act*—requires covered employers to implement certain policies to restrict employee drug use
- *Americans with Disabilities Act*—prohibits discrimination based on disabilities
- *Occupational Safety and Health Act*—establishes safety and health standards for organizations to protect employees
- *Fair Labor Standard Act*—establishes minimum wage and overtime pay
- *Family and Medical Leave Act*—requires employers to provide unpaid leave for childbirth, adoption, illness

EQUIPMENT AND FACILITIES

The third step in the implementation process is to acquire equipment and facilities. In most cases, personnel services are the most expensive budget item. The cost of human resources may be as high as 80 percent. A dollar spent on payroll cannot be amortized, depreciated, or counted as a physical asset. Equipment and facilities also represent high dollar cost items on the budget. Careful planning may avoid the pitfalls of overextension. A lease arrangement, for example, may be an alternative to a purchase. With respect to physical facilities, the location-selection process should receive special attention. For example, area crime rates and availability of services should be researched.

Examples of equipment typically used in a public safety environment include communication equipment, alarm systems, firearms, and vehicles. The quality and expected lifespan of each item in relation to price are a consideration. Competitive bidding, references, and the requirement for performance and service contracts are essential ingredients to successful equipment and facilities acquisitions.

Appropriate alternatives to equipment and facilities lease or purchase should be researched in the planning process. In 1996, for example, white vehicles cost approximately $800 less than multicolored vehicles, and their resale (residual) value was higher. In addition, rear-wheel-drive vehicles are more durable and have a longer lifespan than do front-wheel-drive vehicles when used in hilly terrain. Many police departments and security patrol companies that experimented with front-wheel-drive vehicles have returned to the use of rear-wheel-drive vehicles.

POLICY STATEMENTS

The fourth step to implementation is development of policy statements. In essence, written policies and procedures provide uniform guidelines for handling various types of situations. Policy statements typically describe how anticipated situations should be handled or are written in response to an incident that has occurred but for which there is no existing policy. Policy statements may be many and varied. They may focus on a wide range of personnel issues, such as selection, discipline, promotion, and termination. They also focus on behavioral issues such as chemical abuse, sexual harassment, discrimination, and use of force. They may deal with the process through which day-to-day operations are carried out, as in the form of a Standard Operating Procedures (SOP) manual. Most existing organizations already have numerous policy statements in place. However, these policies must be rewritten to accommodate new variables, and additional policies may be required as new situations arise.

Although policies and their presentation format may vary between organizations, each statement should include at a minimum the following basic items:

- Title of policy statement
- Name of issuing department
- Effective date
- Name of person or persons responsible for approving the policy
- Purpose of the policy stated in clear, concise terms
- The scope of the policy, that is, to whom it applies
- The policy statement itself
- The procedures for implementing the policy
- A list of definitions if uncommon terms are used

CONTRACT SERVICES (OUTSOURCING)

The fifth step in the implementation process involves outsourcing services. If a contract service is appropriate for certain types of services, the following items should be included in the contract:

1. Wage rates versus agency rate specifications. If a premium wage rate (a rate above the prevailing wage) is specified, the contractor should be audited to ensure payment of the premium rate.
2. Insurance coverage specifications. The contractee should consult with an insurance expert to determine the type and amount of insurance to be required of the contractor. Many contractors are underinsured and underfinanced, and they may not have the resources to withstand a lawsuit.
3. Indemnity, hold harmless clause. The client of the contractor is held harmless in the event of a wrongful act by a contract employee.
4. Pre-employment screening (of contract employees). Procedures should be specified in the contract.
5. Audit rights. The client should reserve the right to audit to prevent unscrupulous activities on the part of the contractor.
6. Performance standards and training. These should be included in the contract.
7. Adjustment of compensation clause. The client is allowed to reduce compensation to the contractor for failure to meet obligations spelled out in the contract.

8. Letters of authorization. An outside contractor is authorized to act on behalf of the client agency or corporation. The letters should spell out the contractor's limits of authority.

OPERATIONS

The sixth and final stage in the implementation process is to begin operations. The allocation and deployment of human, financial, and physical resources should be based on need. Too many agencies and businesses allocate resources without giving special attention to where the greatest return on investment may be derived. A careful survey and analysis of high-risk areas and hazards, along with continuous monitoring and evaluation of results, will ensure that the organization receives what it is paying for. When the organization is providing a contracted service, as when a sheriff's department provides police service to a municipality or a contract security company takes over an operation previously serviced by another contractor, the change in service providers should be seamless. In other words, the new contractor should assume responsibilities and duties from the previous contractor without any interruption of service.

REFERENCES

Burstein, H. 1996. *Security: A management perspective.* Englewood Cliffs, N.J.: Prentice-Hall.

Hilgert, R. L., and E. C. Leonard, Jr. 1995. *Supervision: Concepts and practices of management.* 6th ed. Cincinnati: South-Western.

Michelson, R., and P. T. Maher. 1993. *Preparing for promotion: A guide to law enforcement assessment centers.* Blue Lake, Calif.: Innovative Systems-Publishers.

Mosley, D. C., L. D. Megginson, and P. H. Pietri, Jr. 1993. *Supervisory management: The art of empowering and developing people.* Cincinnati: South-Western.

Payton, G. T. and M. Amaral. 1992. *Patrol procedures and enforcement tactics.* San Jose, Calif.: Criminal Justice Services.

Souryal, S. 1981. *Police organization and administration.* San Diego, Calif.: Harcourt Brace Jovanovich.

Chapter 13

Leadership and Ethics

CONCEPTS OF LEADERSHIP

True leadership must be for the benefit of the followers, not the enrichment of the leaders. The universal phenomenon we call leadership has been the subject of a great deal of research from both the theoretical and practical points of view. Leadership has been described variously as a trait, the focus of group process, the art of inducing compliance, the exercise of influence, a kind of behavior or act, a form of persuasion, a power relation, an instrument in goal attainment, an effective interaction, a differentiated role, and an initiation of structure.

Leadership has been defined in terms of acts or behaviors, an act that results in others' acting or responding in a shared direction, the process of arranging a situation to achieve common goals, and the initiation and maintenance of structure in interaction and expectation. It has also been defined as directing and coordinating work relationships while showing consideration, an activity that mobilizes people to do something, and as a social meaning-making process that takes place as a result of activity or work in a group.

Leadership versus Management

Leadership should not be confused with management. Leadership, a concept that is broader than management, occurs anytime one attempts to motivate, influence, or mobilize an individual or group. Management, on the other hand, involves directing people toward organizational goals. Although management and leadership may be exercised or exhibited by the same person, they are distinct concepts. Leadership produces change by establishing direction, aligning people, and motivating and inspiring. Management, on the other hand, brings a measure of order and consistency to organizations by planning and budgeting, organizing and staffing, and controlling.

In considering the distinction between leadership and management, one must examine the following two different courses of life history: (1) development through socialization, which prepares an individual to guide institutions and maintain the existing balance of social relations, and (2) development through personal mastery, which impels an individual to struggle for psychological and social change. Society produces its managerial talent through the first course of life history; leaders emerge through the second course.

Warren Bennis differentiated leadership from management by stating the following:

- The manager administers; the leader innovates.
- The manager is a copy; the leader is an original.
- The manager maintains; the leader develops.
- The manager focuses on systems and structure; the leader focuses on people.
- The manager relies on control; the leader inspires trust.
- The manager has a short-range view; the leader has a long-range perspective.
- The manager asks how and when; the leader asks what and why.
- The manager has an eye on the bottom line; the leader has an eye on the horizon.
- The manager accepts the status quo; the leader challenges it.
- The manager is the classic good soldier; the leader is not a follower.
- The manager does things right; the leader does the right thing.

Theoretical Basis for Leadership

For many years, the most common approach to the study of leadership concentrated on leadership traits. The suggestion was that there were certain characteristics or superior qualities that differentiated leaders from nonleaders. Leadership was explained in terms of traits of personality and character. A review, however, of the research using the trait approach to leadership reveals few significant or consistent findings. Early on, definitions of leadership also viewed the leader as a focus for group change activity and process. According to this view, the leader is always the nucleus of the group.

The work of Fredrick Taylor, a leading theorist of the scientific management movement, has been interpreted as considering people as instruments or machines to be manipulated by their leaders. In essence, the scientific management movement emphasized a concern for output. Sigmund Freud, a psychoanalytical theorist, saw the leader as a father figure, a source of love or fear, as the embodiment of the superego, and as the emotional outlet for followers' frustrations and destructive aggression.

In the 1920s and 1930s the human relations movement held center stage. According to this movement, the organization was to be developed around the workers and had to take into account human feelings and attitudes. The main focus, contrary to the scientific management movement, was on the needs of the individual rather than the needs of the organization.

A leader has been defined as a person who has a program and is moving toward an objective with the group in a definite manner. Others have suggested that leadership involves persuasion and inspiration rather than a direct or implied threat of coercion and that leadership, as a social process, is a social interstimulation that causes people to set out toward an old goal with new zest or a new goal with hopeful courage. In this view, leadership is not the cause of group action but is an effect of it.

J. F. Brown proposed five field-dynamic laws of leadership. According to Brown, leaders must (1) have membership character in the group they are attempting to lead, (2) represent a region of high potential in the social field, (3) adapt themselves to the existing field structure, (4) realize long-term trends in field structure, and (5) recognize that leadership increases in potency at the cost of a reduction in the freedom of leadership.

Barnard (1938) declared that theories of leadership cannot be constructed for behavior in a vacuum. They must contain elements about persons as well as situations. In other words, leadership must focus on the interaction between the situation and the individual. The focus in the situational approach to leadership is on observed behavior not on hypothetical inborn or acquired traits. The effectiveness of a given pattern of leader behavior is actually contingent on the demands imposed by the situation. Understanding a leader's behavior involves exploring the leader's mind to determine what the leader is thinking about the situation in which leadership occurs.

Both trait theorists and situational theorists attempted to explain leadership as an effect of a single set of forces. The interactive effects of individual and situational factors were overlooked. Leadership, therefore, appeared as a manner of interaction involving behavior by and toward an individual who is lifted to a leadership role by other individuals. In this sense leadership is defined in terms of the origination of interaction on the basis of the basic variables of action, interaction, and sentiments. Each participant in this interaction is said to play a role; one person, the leader, influences, and the other persons in the group respond.

The ability to motivate, influence, or persuade has been seen as a step in the direction of defining leadership. Leadership implies influencing change in the conduct of people. Leadership indicates the ability to influence people and secure results through emotional appeals rather than through the exercise of authority. Leadership is the activity of influencing people to cooperate toward a goal they may come to find desirable. Leadership is also the art of dealing with human nature; it is the art of influencing a body of people by example or persuasion to follow a line of action. It is also the process (or act) of influencing activities of an organized group in its efforts toward goal setting and goal achievement.

Tannenbaum and Schmidt (1957) believed that leaders could influence followers by either of two methods. They could tell their followers what to do and how to do it (authoritarian style). Alternatively, they could share their leadership responsibilities with their followers by involving them in the planning and the execution of the task.

Blake and Mouton (1965) conceptualized leadership in terms of a managerial grid in which an individual's concerns for people were compared with that person's concerns for production. An individual who rated high in both areas developed followers who are committed to accomplishing goals in a relationship of trust and respect. Likert (1967) suggested that leaders must take the expectations, values, and interpersonal skills of others into account. Leaders can build group cohesiveness and motivation for productivity by providing freedom for responsible decision making and exercise of initiative.

Hersey and Blanchard (1972) synthesized Blake and Mouton's managerial grid and suggested that leader behavior is related to the maturity of the people being led. They defined maturity in terms of the nonleaders' experience, achievement-motivation, and willingness and ability to accept responsibility. As maturity of nonleaders increased, the leader's involvement decreased.

An important breakthrough in understanding the concept of leadership occurred with the publication of *Leadership* by James MacGregor Burns. Burns (1978) characterized leaders either as transactional (when one person takes the initiative, making contact with others for the purpose of the exchange of valued things) or transformational (when one or more persons engage with others in a way that the leader and nonleader raise one another to higher levels of motivation and morality).

Examples of transactional leadership through a contingent reward approach can be found in *The One Minute Manager* (Blanchard and Johnson 1992). The function of transactional leadership is to maintain the operation of the organization rather than to change it. Transformational leadership, on the other hand, focuses on the three behavior patterns of charisma, intellectual stimulation, and individualized consideration.

Tichy and Ulrich (1984) presented the transformational leader as the model for future leadership excellence. They cited three identifiable activities associated with transformational leadership, as follows: (1) creation of vision—view of future state, (2) mobilization of commitment—acceptance of a new mission, and (3) institutionalization of change—adoption of new patterns of behavior.

Leadership Competencies

Although the study of leadership originally focused on traits or inbred qualities that a person possessed since birth, today it is believed that leadership skills can be acquired or modified extensively through learning. These leadership skills include the skill or competence to keep communication channels open and functioning effectively, interact socially, solve problems, plan, initiate action, and accept responsibility. Also critical to the success of a leader are skills in facilitation of team interaction, effective team problem solving, and training, with substantial attention being paid to the ability to communicate. Such skills are not inherited.

A highly rated leader is likely to be both relations oriented and task oriented, manage conflict successfully, and mobilize and direct individuals toward higher objectives. Successful leaders are willing to negotiate and have a high sense of organizational responsibility. Important in this process is the quality of decision making, commitment, implementation skills, and the ability to use situational strategies. Inability to communicate and relate to other individuals may lead to conflict or incompatibility between the leader and those who are led. Motivational, or person-oriented behaviors, tend to promote follower satisfaction, although they may not contribute to group productivity.

Leadership competencies have been addressed in terms of the ability to plan, organize, and set goals. Leaders must create clear-cut and measurable goals on the basis of advice from all elements of a community. Likert (1961) discovered that high-producing leaders make objectives clear and give people freedom to complete the task. Argyris (1964) suggested that it is in an individual's nature to be self-directed and to seek fulfillment through the exercise of initiative and responsibility. Hersey and Blanchard (1982) suggested that leadership, depending on the situation, involves goal setting, organizing, setting time lines, directing, and controlling.

The functional relation that is leadership exists when a leader is perceived by a group as controlling means for the satisfaction of their needs. Group members make contributions and continue to interact because the members find social exchange mutually rewarding. Changing the expectations of rewards changes the motivation of the individual or the group. A leader can determine followers' perception of the abundance of the rewards available to the followers. Positive reinforcement is used as a means of bringing out desired behavior.

Contemporary Views on Leadership Competencies

Studies have shown that a high-priority leadership attribute is competence (Kouzes and Posner 1993). Contemporary authors often focus on leadership competencies. Bennis (1984, 1993a) identified the four following competencies of leadership:

1. Management of attention—the ability to attract followers
2. Management of meaning—the ability to communicate one's viewpoint or vision
3. Management of trust—reliability
4. Management of self—the ability to know one's skills and use them effectively

Daniel (1992) identified thirteen leadership competencies. They include the following:

1. Goal orientation
2. Bottom-line orientation
3. Communication and enforcement of standards
4. Initiative
5. Strategic influence

6. Communication of confidence
7. Interpersonal sensitivity
8. Development and coaching of others
9. Giving of performance feedback
10. Collaboration and team building
11. Systematic problem solving
12. Image and reputation
13. Self-confidence

Kotter (1993) pointed out that good leaders articulate a vision; involve people in decision making; provide coaching, feedback, and role modeling; and recognize and reward success. Drath and Palus (1994) referred to leadership as a social meaning-making process that takes place as a result of activity or work in a group. They stated that leaders must be trained to participate in, rather than exercise, leadership by learning community-oriented, meaning-making capacities. These capacities include the capacity to understand oneself as both an individual and as a socially embedded being, the capacity to understand systems in general as mutually related and interacting and continually changing, the capacity to appreciate the perspective of another, and the capacity to engage in dialogue.

Leaders must be flexible (Bridges 1994) and demonstrate initiative, integrity, and the ability to empower others (Davids 1995). They must give support, communicate, facilitate interaction, listen actively, and provide feedback (Hersey and Blanchard 1982).

In the final analysis, there is no great divergence in central themes or philosophies regarding leadership, only differences in opinion with respect to the effectiveness of leadership approaches and the application of competencies (Wolfson 1986). The real test of leadership lies in the performance of the groups that are led (Bass 1981), and the competencies required depend on the situation, the people involved, the action to be taken, and the desired results (Byrnbauer and Tyson 1984). In the technologically advanced knowledge society of the future, leadership will be open to, and required of, all workers (Drucker 1994).

In summary, a review of the literature indicates that contemporary leadership requires a philosophy and strategy inconsistent with the traditional models. It suggests that a strategy, or at least a philosophy, that focuses on engagement and solutions to problems can improve the image, efficiency, and effectiveness of public safety and security personnel. This new strategy or philosophy requires that personnel possess a wide variety of technical, cognitive, and affective skills, not the least of which is leadership. The literature also suggests that although as many as eighty generic leadership competencies are identifiable, no clear consensus exists as to what specific competencies are essential to a specific environment. Essentially it depends on the situation. Therefore all personnel should be familiar with the concepts of leadership, how to exercise it, and the differences between leadership and management.

ETHICS

Ethics Defined

Ethics involves a system of moral principles and is concerned with the concept of right and wrong and standards of behavior. Unlike law, which is formally prescribed and enforced by a controlling authority, ethics is based on moral standards, illegal or not. These moral standards, or ethical values, are formed through the influence of others and are concerned with relationships between people and how, ultimately, people live in peace and harmony. Values may be ethical or unethical. Behavior may be unethical but not illegal. Therefore ethics assumes a special meaning and involves the systematic reflection on, and analysis of, morality. It takes on a specific form when someone assumes the roll of a professional.

Theoretical Basis for Ethics

There are two areas of ethical analysis, generally referred to as metaethics and normative ethics. *Metaethical analysis* is an attempt to determine the reasons for making a moral judgment about the moral life. One approach to metaethics is referred to as *absolutism*, whereby unchanging reasons for a course of action are based on knowledge that is considered to be true. The second approach to metaethics is referred to as *relativism*, whereby what is moral, right, or wrong depends on the group or culture within which the behavior takes place.

Normative ethics considers more concrete questions. For example, what types of acts are morally right or wrong? There are two approaches or theories involved in normative ethics. One is referred to as *deontological ethics*, which is duty driven. With this type of approach the means through which one acts count more than the ends. Here one is required to act according to one's duties, rights, and sense of responsibility. The other approach to normative ethics is referred to as *teleological*. This approach is goal driven; ends count, and concern focuses on consequences. The latter is often referred to as the *utilitarian* viewpoint.

Ethics and Professional Conduct

Generally speaking, ethical standards dictate behavior when law or precedents, which may prescribe behavior, do not exist. This means that whenever one possesses the power of discretionary decision-making behavior, the behavior should conform to what one *ought* to do even though law, policy, or precedent prescribing *must-do* behaviors is not available. The ends *do not* always justify the means. Conducting oneself according to an acceptable ethical standard, whether the profession has a code (canon) of ethics or not, means doing the right thing at the right time. From a professional standpoint, this also means avoiding civil and criminal liability for one's actions.

The principles of ethics and the harm each is designed to prevent or correct include the following:

- Nonmaleficence (refraining from harming oneself or another) occurs when an individual or organization is in a position potentially to destroy or otherwise harm someone else.
- Beneficence (bringing about good) occurs when an individual or organization is in a position to benefit someone else.
- Fidelity (promise keeping) occurs when an individual or organization has made a promise, explicit or implicit, to someone else.
- Veracity occurs when an individual or organization is in a position to tell the truth or deceive someone.
- Justice occurs when an individual or organization is in a position to distribute benefits and burdens among individuals or groups in society who have legitimate claims on the benefits.
- Reparations occurs when an individual or organization has wronged someone else and made amends for the wrong.
- Gratitude occurs when an individual or organization has been the beneficiary of someone else's kindness.
- Confidentiality occurs when an individual or organization is in a position to harm someone with inappropriate disclosure of information.

Potential ethical problems in public safety and security include corruption, discrimination, violation of rights to privacy, violation of rights under the Constitution, entrapment, negligence, illicit business practices, excessive use of force, and uncivil conduct. Each of these areas should be addressed in new-employee and in-service training programs. The "ends justify the means" is inconsistent with professional ethics.

REFERENCES

Argyris, C. 1964. *Integrating the individual and the organization.* New York: Wiley.
Barnard, C. I. 1938. *The functions of the executive.* Cambridge, Mass.: Harvard University Press.
Bass, B. M. 1981. *Stogdill's handbook of leadership: A survey of theory and research.* New York: The Free Press.
Bennis, W. G. 1984. The four competencies of leadership. *Training and Development Journal* 38 (September): 14–19.
Bennis, W. G. 1993a. *An invented life: Reflections on leadership and change.* Reading, Mass.: Addison-Wesley.
Bennis, W. G. 1993b. *Managing the dream: Leadership in the 21st century.* In *Contemporary issues in leadership*, 3rd ed., edited by W. E. Rosenbach and R. L. Taylor. Boulder, Colo.: Westview Press.

Blake, R. R., and J. S. Mouton. 1965. A 9.9 approach for increasing organizational productivity. In *Personal and organizational change through group methods*, edited by E. H. Schein and W. G. Bennis. New York: Wiley.

Blanchard, K., and S. Johnson. 1992. *The one minute manager.* New York: Morrow.

Bridges, W. 1994. The end of the job. *Fortune* September 19, 64.

Brown, J. F. 1936. *Psychology and the social order.* New York: McGraw-Hill.

Bunning, R. L. 1979. The Delphi technique: A projection tool for serious inquiry. In *The 1979 annual handbook for group facilitators.* San Diego: University Associates.

Burns, J. M. 1978. *Leadership.* New York: Harper & Row.

Burns, L. R., and S. W. Becker. 1988. Leadership and decision making. In *Health care management: A text in organization theory and behavior*, edited by S. M. Shortell and A. D. Kaluzny. 2nd ed. New York: Wiley.

Byrnbauer, H., and L. A. Tysen. 1984. Flexing the muscles of technical leadership. *Training and Development Journal* 38 (September): 48–52.

Daniel T. 1992. Identifying critical leadership competencies of manufacturing supervisors in a major electronics corporation. *Group and Organizational Management: An International Journal* 17 No. 1 (March): 57–71.

Davids, M. 1995. Where style meets substance. *Journal of Business Strategy* 16 No. 1 (January-February): 57–60.

Drath, W. H., and C. J. Paulus. 1994. *Making common sense: Leadership as meaning-making in a community of practice.* Greensboro, N.C.: Center for Creative Leadership.

Drucker, P. F. 1994. The age of social transformation. *The Atlantic Monthly* November, 53–80.

Hersey, P., and K. H. Blanchard. 1972. The management of change: change and the use of power. *Training Development Journal* 26: 6–10.

Hersey, P., and K. H. Blanchard. 1982. *Management of organizational behavior: Utilizing human resources.* Englewood Cliffs, N.J.: Prentice-Hall.

Kotter, J. P. 1993. What leaders really do. In *Contemporary issues in leadership*, edited by W. E. Rosenbach and R. L. Taylor. Boulder, Colo.: Westview Press.

Kouzes, J. M., and B. Z. Posner. 1993. The credibility factor: What people expect of leaders. In *Contemporary issues in leadership.* 3rd ed, edited by W. E. Rosenbach and R. L. Taylor. Boulder, Colo.: Westview Press.

Likert, R. 1961. *New patterns of management.* New York: McGraw-Hill.

Likert, R. 1967. *The human organization.* New York: McGraw-Hill.

Ortmeier, P. J. 1996. *Community policing leadership: A Delphi study to identify essential competencies.* Ann Arbor: UMI Dissertation Services.

Tannenbaum, R., and W. H. Schmidt. 1957. How to choose a leadership pattern. *Harvard Business Review* 34 (March-April): 95–101.

Taylor, F. W. 1911. *The principles of scientific management.* New York: Harper and Brothers.

Tichy, N., and D. Ulrich. 1984. The leadership challenge: A call for the transformational leader. SMR Forum. *Sloan Management Review* 26: 59–68.

Wolfson, P. G. 1986. *The perceptions of corporate executives and member company general managers concerning the competencies essential for agribusiness leaders.* Carbondale: Southern Illinois University.

Chapter 14

Evaluation

In the 1960s, Robert Townsend took the reins of an international rent-a-car company named Avis. The company had not made a profit in the thirteen years of its life. Three years after Townsend's arrival, Avis profits were up to $9 million dollars. Townsend's philosophy was simple: Hire the right people and treat them fairly, solicit employee and consumer input in decision making, eliminate excuses for failure, and strive for excellence.

Excellence does not develop on its own. To achieve excellence in any organization, special attention must be given to the evaluation process. Even the most carefully developed plans may fail without evaluation of progress and results. After a plan has been implemented, evaluation and control begin. This process is exercised continuously throughout the life of the operation. The process involves measuring performance, comparing performance with stated objectives, reporting results, and taking corrective action, if necessary. As such, the process involves follow-up and is closely aligned with planning. In essence, evaluation involves a return to the first step of the planning process—needs assessment.

Evaluation has forward-looking and after-the-fact aspects. Through the forward-looking aspect, the evaluators attempt to anticipate and prevent potential sources of deviation from established standards and consider the possibility of undesirable outcomes. Crime prevention is an example of forward-looking evaluation. After-the-fact evaluation is analysis of why an event or deviation from established standards has occurred and is used to determine the corrective action required. Determining the cause of a rash of reported burglaries in a particular neighborhood is an example of after-the-fact evaluation.

MEASURING PERFORMANCE

The first step in the evaluation and control process is to measure performance on the basis of the objectives established during the planning process. These objectives, or standards, are units of measurement that serve as reference points for evaluating results. Standards can be either tangible or intangible. *Tangible standards* are quite clear, concrete, specific, identifiable, and generally measurable. These standards are used to measure quantity and quality of output. They may be used to assess the impact of a budget or appraise individual employee performance.

Tangible standards can be categorized as numerical, monetary, physical, or time related. Numerical standards are expressed in numbers, such as number of items produced, number of absences, percentage of successful calls, or number of personnel who successfully complete training. Monetary standards are expressed in dollars and cents. Examples of monetary standards are predetermined profit margins in private businesses, payroll costs, and maintenance costs. Physical standards refer to quality, durability, size, weight, or other factors related to physical composition. Time standards refer to the speed with which a job should be done.

Intangible standards are not expressed in terms of numbers, money, physical qualities, or time, because they relate to human characteristics that are difficult to measure. They take no physical form. Yet they are just as important as tangible standards. Examples of intangible standards are a desirable attitude, high morale, ethics, cooperation, and the reputation of the organization.

Performance may be measured through personal observation; written or oral reports of subordinates; automatic methods; and inspections, tests, or surveys. Some members of the organization may resent performance measurement. This resentment may result from the use of efficiency experts and supervisors who set unrealistic standards of performance. Managers within an organization must remember that performance standards should be based on realistic targets.

COMPARING PERFORMANCE WITH STANDARDS

Failure to meet a performance standard may be the result of a variety of causes. Identification of the cause rather than the symptoms is extremely important if appropriate corrective action is to be taken. It is important to consult with those closest to the situation to determine *why* the performance standards are not being met. Participation of all affected members of the organization is an essential ingredient in this process. Time also is essential to the evaluation process. The sooner a deviation from a standard is identified, the sooner the situation can be corrected. Evaluation and assessment, therefore, must be a continuous process.

TAKING CORRECTIVE ACTION

If no deviations from an established standard occur, the evaluative check has been fulfilled. However, after a careful analysis of any deviation from a performance standard, corrective action may be necessary. Modifications, adjustments, and alterations of the original plan should not be viewed negatively. After all, objectives and standards as stated in the original plan often are based on forecasts. If the deviation from the standard is extreme or exceptional, it may be necessary to evaluate the planning process itself.

Before taking any corrective action it should be noted that there may be many reasons why a deviation from an established standard has occurred. These reasons may include the following:

1. The standards could not be achieved because they were based on faulty forecasts or assumptions or because an unforeseen problem arose that distorted the anticipated results.
2. Failure has occurred in another job (or activity) that preceded the job in question.
3. The employee who performed the job either was unqualified or was not given adequate directions or instructions.
4. The employee who performed the job was negligent or did not follow required directions or procedures.

Therefore, before any corrective action is taken, the actual causes of the deviation should be analyzed carefully. Knee-jerk reactions may cause greater harm to occur.

QUALITY ASSURANCE

Quality can be an elusive concept. It means different things to different people. In the context of assuring consumer satisfaction, quality may be defined as a phenomenon associated with products, people, services, processes, and environments that meet or exceed expectations. Quality assurance, continuous quality improvement, and total quality management (TQM) initiatives involve approaches to administration that attempt to maximize effectiveness (or competitiveness) of an organization through continual improvement of the quality of its people, processes, products, and environment. Quality assurance initiatives should involve everyone in the organization, as well as consumers, in the process of identifying and improving every aspect of the organization. These initiatives should be based on the following:

- Decisions founded on facts rather than intuition
- Taking personal responsibility for quality
- Improving teamwork and commitment
- A focus on the end user and service

Quality initiatives also involve goal setting, trust, building cohesion, developing problem-solving skills, increasing information flow, and resolving conflict. At a minimum, a total quality assurance approach includes the following ingredients:

- Customer focus (internal and external)
- Obsession with quality
- Use of the scientific approach in decision making and problem solving

- Long-term commitment
- Teamwork
- Employee involvement and empowerment
- Continual improvement
- Bottom-up education and training
- Freedom through control
- Unity of purpose

Quality assurance initiatives are not a quick fix. Rather, they are an entirely new approach to administration that requires new management styles, long-term commitments, unity of purpose, and specialized training.

COMMON ERRORS WITH QUALITY INITIATIVES

In addition to making half-hearted implementation efforts and having unrealistic expectations, organizations commonly make several other errors when starting quality initiatives. These include the following.

Senior Management Delegation and Poor Leadership

Some organizations attempt to start a quality initiative by delegating responsibility to a hired expert rather than applying the leadership necessary to get everyone involved.

Team Mania

Teams should be established. However, working in teams is an approach that must be learned. Supervisors must learn how to be effective coaches, and employees must learn how to be team players. The organization must undergo a cultural change before teamwork can succeed. Rushing in and putting everyone on teams before learning has occurred and the corporate culture has changed will create problems rather than solve them.

Deployment Process Errors

Some organizations develop quality initiatives without concurrently developing plans for integrating them into all elements of the organization. The focus must be on total, not partial, quality management.

Taking a Narrow, Dogmatic Approach

None of the approaches proposed by leading quality experts is truly a one-size-fits-all proposition. Even the experts encourage organizations to tailor quality programs to individual needs.

Confusion about the Differences between Education, Awareness, Inspiration, and Skill Building

One can send people to days of training in group dynamics, inspire them, teach them managerial styles, and show them all sorts of grids and analyses, but that does not mean they have developed any skills. There is a time to educate and inspire and make people aware, and there is a time to give them practical tools they can use to do something specific and different from what they have done in the past. To reach quality assurance goals, organizations must focus on all of the essential ingredients to success in implementing quality initiatives.

According to Goetsch and Davis (1995), quality assurance initiatives should include the following steps:

1. Commit to total quality
2. Form a total quality steering committee
3. Build teams
4. Provide total quality training
5. Create the vision and guiding principles
6. Set broad objectives
7. Communicate and publicize
8. Identify strengths and weaknesses
9. Identify advocates and resisters
10. Assess baseline employee attitudes
11. Assess baseline customer satisfaction
12. Plan the implementation approach
13. Identify projects
14. Establish team composition
15. Train the teams
16. Activate and direct the teams
17. Give feedback to steering committee
18. Give feedback to customers
19. Give feedback to employees
20. Modify the infrastructure as necessary

It is a long-established fact that human beings are resistant to change. Public safety and security personnel are no exception. The injection of quality assurance and assessment initiatives into the public safety and security areas has resulted in a marked change in the way many agencies and firms conduct business. Attitudes do not change overnight. Nor do they change without reasonable justification for change. Concrete evidence of the benefits of quality assurance initiatives may be the only way to enlighten and persuade public safety and security personnel that quality service is what helps to gain public and consumer trust and support for the organization and the people in it.

REFERENCES

Clemmer, J. 1992. 5 common errors companies make starting quality initiatives. *Total Quality* 3 (April): 7.

Craig, D. P. 1978. *Hip pocket guide to planning and evaluation.* San Diego: University Associates.

Goetsch, D. L., and S. Davis. 1995. *Implementing total quality.* Englewood Cliffs, N.J.: Prentice-Hall.

Haberer, J. B., and M. L. W. Webb. 1994. *TQM: 50 ways to make it work for you.* Menlo Park, Calif.: Crisp Publications.

Hilgert, R. L., and E. C. Leonard, Jr. 1995. *Supervision: Concepts and practices of management.* Cincinnati: South-Western.

Mosley, D. C., L. C. Megginson, and P. H. Pietri. 1993. *Supervisory management: The art of empowering and developing people.* Cincinnati: South-Western.

Silberman, M., ed. 1996. *The 1996 McGraw-Hill team and organization development source book.* New York: McGraw-Hill.

Townsend, R. 1970. *Up the organization.* New York: Fawcett Crest.

Part Four

Collateral Functions

Chapter 15

Investigations

Simply stated, an investigation may be defined as any systematic inquiry to determine the facts surrounding an event or situation. Investigations typically are warranted when an accident or unexplained loss occurs or when alleged individual misconduct or criminal activity is reported. From a business standpoint, a well-documented investigation is probably the best defense against claims of unlawful employment discrimination and wrongful termination.

Investigation is an art as well as a science. The competencies and attributes of good investigators include the following:

1. Excellent verbal and written communication skills
2. Excellent human-relations skills
3. Knowledge of civil and criminal law
4. Knowledge of the judicial process
5. Research, analytical, and critical thinking skills
6. Problem-solving skills

The purpose of any investigation essentially is to determine the following:

1. What happened?
2. Who was involved?
3. Where did it happen?
4. When did it happen?
5. How did it happen? — *primary focus*
6. Why did it happen? —

INVESTIGATION: COMMON ELEMENTS

The common elements of any investigation include the following:

1. Identification of the problem, issue, or situation
2. Identification of the essential facts to be acquired and proved
3. Identification of potential sources and locations of information
4. Selection of an efficient investigative method

5. Location and preservation of information and evidence
6. Reevaluation and reinvestigation, if necessary

SOURCES OF INFORMATION

Sources of information for an investigation typically include victims, witnesses, records, and informants. The most important aspect of any investigation is interviewing of victims and witnesses. Each should be interviewed thoroughly and as soon as possible after the incident occurs.

Public records may include local, state, and federal police and other government records. Private individual and business records and various publications may be invaluable sources of information. Access to records may be gained through permission, the legal process, or the records may be accessible as the result of their status as public records. Department of Motor Vehicles (DMV) records, real property ownership and transfers, and criminal conviction data are typically a matter of public record and accessible by anyone. Arrest data may be accessible by criminal justice agencies only.

Informants are an important source of information. They are indispensable in many criminal investigations. When informants are used, care should be exercised to evaluate their motives and the information provided to ensure reliability. In a criminal prosecution, the reliability of informant information is critical. Failure to test the reliability of informant-supplied information can result in the inadmissibility of any evidence derived therefrom.

GENERAL INVESTIGATIVE METHODS

Investigative methods include interviewing, interrogation, instrumentation, and surveillance. Any or all of these methods may be used during the course of a single investigation.

Oral (or testimonial) information is derived from victims, witnesses, and subjects (suspects) of an investigation. Victims, witnesses, and subjects are interviewed. Suspects to a crime are interrogated. Interviews typically should be conducted in a environment that makes the interviewee feel comfortable to reduce nervousness and encourage a free flow of information. Interrogations, on the other hand, should be conducted in an environment foreign to the suspect. A rights advisory, according to the Miranda decision of 1966, is not required in the private sector.

Instrumentation refers to the application of the physical sciences to the investigative process. These sciences include physics, chemistry, biology, anatomy, and physiology. Surveillance, or as it is referred to in private business, subrosa, involves the direct observation of persons, places, or things. Observation methods include spot checks, stationary plants, and moving surveillance.

CIVIL INVESTIGATIONS

The types of civil investigations are many and varied. Businesses and individuals may conduct investigations that focus on noncriminal events and activities. Examples of civil investigations and methods include the following.

Background Investigations

Background investigations are typically conducted as part of pre-employment screening of prospective employees. Businesses and agencies may be able to prevent the hiring of a liability if a "due diligence" background investigation is conducted. In addition, companies and agencies may wish to investigate the background of other organizations with whom a business relationship is sought.

Personal Injury and Property Damage

Collision and accident investigations always should be conducted when a personal injury is involved. Procedurally it may be necessary to reconstruct the event to determine the exact cause or causes. Not all collisions are accidents. Some are intentional. Likewise, not all "accidents" are unintentional.

Worker Compensation Claims

There are two general types of worker compensation claims. Each requires a thorough investigation. The first category includes those injuries that have arisen out of employment (AOE). AOE injuries are those that have developed over a long period of time, such as stress or lung disease. The other category involves injuries occurring during the course of employment (COE). COE injuries occur within the scope of employment and may be attributed to a single event or act, such as a fall.

Insurance Investigation

Investigations conducted by or for insurance companies are numerous and varied. These investigations may focus on personal injury, property damage, AOE or COE worker compensation claims, collisions, accidents, fraud, or any other situation in which the insurance company may be financially liable.

Sexual Harassment

Employers are required by law to investigate claims of sexual harassment. Failure to investigate thoroughly and take corrective action when there is a factual basis for the allegation may result in a legal liability. For example, in 1994, a prestigious law firm sustained a judgment of $7.1 million against it for failing to take appropriate action in a case of sexual harassment.

Employment Discrimination

Employers are required by law to investigate claims of unlawful employment discrimination. This includes claims of discrimination on the basis of age, sex, race, ethnicity, or disability.

Wrongful Termination

Wrongful termination may involve discriminatory action on the part of an employer or may result from a false accusation of dishonesty or chemical abuse. In the case of a lawsuit, the former employee often attacks the employer's investigation as inadequate, superficial, or an outright witch hunt. Today discharge requires proof of sufficient cause and meticulous documentation of the history of wrongdoing by the employee and warnings given and action taken by the employer.

Chemical Abuse

Employees under the influence of chemicals are less productive than other employees, do poor-quality work, have poor attendance, and pose safety hazards. A key factor in handling those who abuse chemicals is to recognize the symptoms and take corrective action through counseling, referral, discipline, and possibly, termination.

Any Unexplained Loss

Any unexplained loss to the agency or business should be investigated. The results may be used as the foundation for corrective action to prevent future occurrences. If it is determined that the loss is the result of criminal activity, information (evidence) gathered during the course of a thorough investigation may be used to prosecute the offender.

SPECIAL ISSUES IN CIVIL INVESTIGATIONS

Several issues arise in the course of an investigation in a private business or organization. These include privacy issues surrounding searches, surreptitious (secret) investigative methods, and the use of a polygraph. Another issue involves the use of detention.

Searches

Searches of desks, lockers, and other areas under the direct control of employees or others raise serious questions regarding the right to privacy. If work areas are to be searched (or inspected) it is important to give employees clear, prior, written notice that such searches may occur. The policy with respect to searches should be contained in an employee handbook and posted prominently in work areas. It generally is inadvisable to search a locked desk drawer or locker of an employee without the employee's consent. The physical search of a person generally is *not permissible.*

Surreptitious (Secret) Investigative Methods

Many statutory provisions severely restrict the ability of an employer to use surreptitious (secret) investigative methods. These methods include the use of electronic monitoring (wiretapping), eavesdropping, and undercover investigators. Few definitive court rulings describe the limits (if any) of any employer's monitoring of employees by electronic means (other than eavesdropping on telephone conversations). Several invasion of privacy actions, however, have been filed against employers who have monitored electronic mail or similar messages being transmitted between employees. Federal legislation that affects electronic monitoring in the workplace includes the following:

- *Omnibus Crime Control and Safe Streets Act of 1968.*
  A federal appeals court has held that an employer violated the federal Omnibus Crime Control and Safe Streets Act of 1968 by recording telephone calls made by employees on a store telephone. The U.S. Eighth Circuit Court of Appeals relied on a 1986 amendment to the Omnibus Crime Control and Safe Streets Act. That provision of the act contains an exemption only for "system providers," such as employers, who provide electronic communication systems.
- The *Privacy of Consumers and Workers Act.* Two similar pieces of proposed legislation have been introduced in Congress that would greatly reduce electronic surveillance or monitoring of employees. Both bills are referred to as the Privacy of Consumers and Workers Act. This act, if passed, would require each employer who engages in electronic monitoring to provide all affected employees with prior, written notice that such monitoring may take place. The notice must include the forms of electronic monitoring to be used, the personal data to be collected, the frequency of each form of electronic monitoring that will occur, and the use of personal data collected.

Under the act, if an employer decides to conduct electronic monitoring, the employer would be required to provide the affected employee and customers with a signal light, beeping tone, verbal notification, or other form of visual or audio notice, at periodic intervals, to indicate electronic monitoring is taking place. Employers would also be required to give employees access to all personal data obtained. An employer would not be able to use the personal data obtained by means of electronic monitoring as the exclusive basis for individual employee performance evaluation or disciplinary action. Any employer who violates the act would be subject to a civil penalty of up to $10,000.

Many states have or are considering laws which severely restrict an employer's ability to monitor employees. California employers, for example, are prohibited from eavesdropping on confidential employee communication. A confidential communication includes any communication carried on in circumstances reasonably indicating that any party to the communication desires it to be confined to the parties thereto. The term does not include communication made in a public gathering. It also does not apply to any public utility engaged in the business of providing communication services. California Penal Code provisions that pertain to eavesdropping on confidential communication include the following:

• Penal Code Section 630. States that the use of devices for the purpose of eavesdropping equates to an invasion of privacy.
• Penal Code Section 631. Defines eavesdropping as intentionally tapping or making any unauthorized connection, whether physically, electronically, or otherwise, or willfully and without the consent of all parties to the communication or in any unauthorized manner reading or attempting to read or learn the contents or meaning of any message, report, or other communication.
• Liability for Violating Penal Code Section 631. Sanctions for violation of Section 631 include a fine, not to exceed $2,500, or imprisonment, not to exceed 1 year. Employers should note that any evidence obtained in violation of PC631 is inadmissible in any judicial, administrative, legislative, or other proceeding. Accordingly, even if an employer uncovers significant information about the employee, the employer will not be able to use such information.
• Penal Code Section 632. Prohibits the recording by means of any electronic amplifying or recording device whether the communication is carried on among such parties in the presence of one another or by means of a telephone or other device.

These penal code provisions place severe restrictions on the ability of an employer to monitor employee performance. A suggestion is to give employees advance, written notice of such monitoring. Employers should ensure that employees have given their full and voluntary consent in writing. Readers should consult their respective state and local laws regarding surreptitious investigative methods.

At present, there are no definitive reported cases limiting an employer's right to conduct a legitimate undercover investigation. Undercover investigations are most appropriate when an employer suspects theft or illegal drug activity is actually operating within the employer's facility.

Polygraphs and Voice Stress Analyzers

State and federal law both place severe restrictions on the use of polygraphs or similar devices by private employers. The federal statute contains a general exception for ongoing investigations involving economic loss. There also are exceptions under the federal law for employers in specific industries. Significant provisions of state and federal law include the following:

- *California Labor Code Section 432.2.* Prohibits employers from demanding or requiring that any applicant or employee take a polygraph test, a "lie detector" test, or any other similar test or examination as a condition of employment or as a condition of continued employment.
- *Employee Polygraph Protection Act* (federal). Prohibits employers from directly or indirectly requiring, requesting, suggesting, or causing any employee or prospective employee to take or submit to any lie detector test; using, accepting, referring to, or inquiring about the results of any lie detector test; and discharging, disciplining, discriminating against, or denying employment or promotion to, or threatening any such action against, any employee or prospective employee who refuses, declines, or fails to take a lie detector test. An employer may not base an employment decision on the results of any lie detector test. Under the Employee Polygraph Protection Act, a lie detector includes a polygraph, voice stress analyzer, psychological stress evaluator, or any other similar device.

Exemptions under the Federal Polygraph Act are as follows:

1. Government exemption. The Employee Polygraph Protection Act does not apply to the U.S. government or any state or any local government. The act also does not apply to the federal government in the performance of any counterintelligence function or any lie detector test given to employees of private employers who have contracts with the Department of Defense.
2. Private employer investigative exemption. A private employer may request an employee to take a polygraph test if all of the following conditions are met:
   - The test is administered in connection with an ongoing investigation involving economic loss to the employer's business
   - The employee had access to the property

- The employer has reasonable suspicion that the employee was involved
- The employer executes a statement giving fair notice

3. Security service exemption. The federal act does not prohibit the use of a polygraph test by private employers whose primary business consists of providing armored car personnel, security system personnel, or other security personnel.

4. Drug security, drug theft, or drug division investigations exemption. The federal act does not prohibit use of a polygraph test by an employer authorized to manufacture, distribute, or dispense certain controlled substances.

5. Restrictions on the use of exemptions. The employer investigation exemption shall not apply if an employee is discharged, disciplined, denied employment or promotion, or otherwise discriminated against in any manner on the basis of the analysis of a polygraph test chart or refusal to take a polygraph test unless there is additional supporting evidence. Under the exemption for security services, drug security, drug theft, or similar investigation, an employer may not use the results as the sole basis for an adverse employment action. Furthermore, during the actual testing phase, the examiner may not ask any questions that were not presented in writing for review to the examinee before the test. Finally, a private employer may disclose information from a test only to the examinee or any other persons specifically designated in writing by the examinee or any court.

Unlawful Detention

Unlawful detention issues may arise whenever someone's freedom of movement is restricted in a significant way. Unless a person is placed under criminal or civil (citizen's) arrest, it is unlawful to detain that person against his or her will. Unlawful detention can result in criminal and civil liability for false imprisonment or false arrest.

CRIMINAL INVESTIGATIONS

Overview

The purposes of a criminal investigation are to determine whether a crime was committed; identify the suspect; locate the suspect; and recognize, collect, and preserve evidence that may establish guilt (or innocence) of the accused in a judicial proceeding. A criminal investigation may be considered successful if all available physical evidence is collected and preserved properly, witnesses have been intelligently interviewed, the suspect, if willing, has been effectively interrogated, all leads are properly developed, and the investigation is reported properly.

Was a Crime Committed?

As mentioned in Chapter 3, the importance of knowing the law cannot be overemphasized. This is particularly true with respect to criminal law. The first step in a criminal investigation is to determine whether a crime was committed and if so, what type of crime. Criminal, or penal, codes specifically describe what behavior is criminal. Each element of an offense must be established in the incident under investigation for a crime to have occurred. Furthermore, the powers to arrest, of both a police officer and a private citizen, differ depending on whether the crime was a felony or misdemeanor. Failure to know the law may result in civil, and possibly criminal, liability for false arrest or false imprisonment.

Identification of the Perpetrator

The identification of a suspected perpetrator may be accomplished in one of several ways. First, the suspect may be apprehended at the scene or provide the investigator with an admission or confession. Second, eyewitnesses to the crime may be available. Third, circumstantial evidence in the form of motive, opportunity to commit the crime, or trace evidence that can associate, or place, the suspect with the crime scene may be available.

Locating the Perpetrator

If the suspect is not present at the crime scene, it will be necessary to trace and locate the suspect. Crime suspects usually are not in hiding. Rather, their whereabouts are simply unknown. However, locating and apprehending a suspect may require persistence. A systematic procedure enhances the possibility of apprehending a suspect.

Before launching a search for a fugitive, the investigator should be certain that the legal requirements for a possible arrest have been satisfied and that all pertinent background information and identification data on the suspect have been gathered. The investigator should collect as much information as possible regarding the suspect's history. Criminal records, if available, provide information regarding aliases used, location of previous arrests and convictions, arresting agencies, the nature of previous offenses, and fingerprints. Other forms of trace data include telephone, city, and criss-cross directories; credit bureaus; motor vehicle records; identification data from immigration, passport, or military records; informants; county assessors and recorders offices; past friends and acquaintances; union halls; blood banks; and lodging establishments.

Collection and Preservation of Physical Evidence

In addition to the elements of interviewing and interrogation discussed previously and documentation and report writing discussed in Chapter 16, criminal investigation may involve instrumentation and adherence to strict procedures used in the identification, collection, and preservation of physical evidence at a crime scene.

On arrival at the scene of a crime, the first responder should check the physical condition of the victim, if present, to determine whether medical assistance is required. Second, witnesses to the incident should be retained for questioning. Third, the scene itself should be secured to prevent tampering with evidence until appropriate personnel arrive to process the scene. If a crime scene search is warranted, the search should be organized. Methods of searching include strip, grid, spiral, and zone techniques. Physical evidence collected at a crime scene should be photographed, entered into the crime scene sketch, collected, and preserved to maintain legal integrity. This essentially involves careful marking or labeling of the evidence for future identification, protection of the evidence from contamination, and maintenance of the chain of custody of the evidence.

THE INVESTIGATOR AS A WITNESS

Investigators often are called as witnesses to testify in a criminal or civil proceeding or to provide a deposition to be used in the judicial process. It is extremely important for the investigator to prepare for such testimony. Notes, reports, and evidence should be reviewed to refresh the investigator's memory. Consulting with the attorney for whom the investigator will be testifying also is necessary. The attorney may point out weak points in the preparation for court. Finally, during the judicial proceeding, the investigator as a witness should always remain alert and present a professional appearance and demeanor. Professionalism adds to the credibility of the witness.

REFERENCES

State of California. *Labor Code*, §432.2.
State of California. *Penal Code*, §630–632.
United States Congress. *Omnibus Crime Control and Safe Streets Act*. Public Law 90–351, Title 18 U.S.C. §2518, 1968.
United States Congress. *Employee Polygraph Protection Act*. Public Law 100–347, Title 29 U.S.C. §2001–2009, 1988.

Chapter 16

Documentation and Report Writing

Paper is our most important product! This statement is especially true when it is necessary to document the facts surrounding an incident, interview, accident, or crime. Probably no other single activity in business or public endeavor is more important (or falls lower on the priority list) than the need for effective documentation, comprehensive notes, and quality reports.

METHODS FOR RECORDING INFORMATION

Documentation typically is accomplished through traditional note-taking and report-writing methods. If physical, technical, and legal requirements permit, recording may be made through the use of audiotape, videotape, stenography, or computer-assisted recording devices. If computers are used to generate notes and reports, care should be taken to ensure that confidentiality is maintained and access is restricted to a need-to-know basis. For example, computer disks that have been erased retain information that can be retrieved through a process called *degaussing*. In addition, other electronic media, such as E-mail and the Internet, are not secure from message interception by outsiders.

NOTES

As a rule, notes should be made contemporaneously with the incident and refer to documentation made during the course of the activity or immediately after an incident occurs. Because memories fade and are often imperfect, notes should be written and maintained in the normal course of one's occupation. Therefore, pen and parchment may be the most important tools in the world of work. Notes are personal to the note taker and may be used as follows:

1. To refresh one's memory
2. As the foundation for an official report

3. As supporting evidence (Example: Notes routinely recorded during telephone conversations may be used as evidence to support the fact that the conversation took place and attest to the content of the conversation.)

Although notes are generally written for the note taker's consumption, caution should be exercised when writing notes, because any recording may be subject to review by another person, business, agency, or in a judicial proceeding.

REPORTS

Unlike notes, reports are typically generated for public consumption. Reports may become part of an official record that forms the foundation for history. Reports may be viewed by other employees, supervisors, the news media, social service agencies, attorneys, the police, and the courts. They may be scrutinized in the judicial process, provide evidence for litigation against the report writer, or support a defense against a lawsuit or criminal charge. They are used to determine future courses of action and as the basis for promotion, discipline, and evaluation. It is readily apparent, then, that reports can have negative as well as positive consequences and should be taken seriously. Reports with misspelled words, poor grammar and punctuation, and inaccuracies or omissions are potentially costly. Defective reports also cast doubt on the professionalism of the report writer.

Reports vary in form and content. All reports, however, have one common purpose, that is, to communicate information in a clear, concise, and accurate manner. Reports should always be written with the audience or potential readers in mind. In essence, effective report writing is a matter of reducing to writing the pertinent facts concerning an issue or event in much the same way and in much the same order that a story would be told orally.

TYPES OF REPORTS

The following are types of reports:

1. Contact reports—used to document information acquired during any contact with another person or persons
2. Incident or crime reports—used to document the occurrence of an event or reported criminal activity
3. Narrative or supplemental reports—used to narrate what happened, record witness statements, and record additional information acquired subsequent to an original report
4. Accident or traffic collision reports—used to record the circumstances surrounding an accident or vehicle collision

5. Agency- or business-specific reports—used for routine reports that are written or completed in the normal course of business; may include inspection and audit reports or surveys
6. Memoranda and business letters—used for general interdepartmental and interbusiness or interagency communication

The types of reports used by an agency or business depend on the nature of the activity of the organization and its documentation requirements. Most existing organizations have reporting forms and formats in place. New agencies or businesses seeking to develop report forms and procedures should consult with similar existing organizations for information. Many publishers market report form books and computer software packages.

REPORT WRITING

General Principles

To be considered acceptable, a report must meet the following criteria:

1. The writing must be reasonably fluent, well developed, and well organized and show sufficient command of the language to communicate the information.
2. All essential information must be included in the report (who, what, where, when, how, why)
3. The report must be free of mechanical errors (typing, grammar, punctuation, spelling, and word choice) that diminish its evidentiary value or usefulness.
4. The time required to complete the report must be reasonable and consistent with the expectations of the job.

Specific Guidelines

The following guidelines are critical to effective report writing. The writer should do the following:

1. Conduct a proper inquiry into the subject material of the intended report
2. Take complete, accurate, readable notes
3. Use the proper format, depending on for whose use the report is intended
4. Choose the correct language
5. Use proper sentence structure
6. Be completely accurate with all the facts
7. Do not omit facts
8. Differentiate facts from hearsay, conclusions, judgments, and personal opinions

9. Strive for clarity
10. Be concise
11. Be absolutely fair
12. Be complete
13. Record the sequence of events in chronologic order
14. Record the names, addresses, and, if possible, social security or identification numbers of all involved
15. Include an introduction, body, and conclusion in all narratives
16. Check spelling, punctuation, and capitalization
17. Review the report to ensure that it adequately answers the questions who, what, when, where, how, and why

Parts of a Report

Sometimes a specific report form may not be available. To ensure that a report is complete, the report writer should strive to include the following information in the report:

1. Administrative data, including the date of the report, file or case number (if applicable), subjects involved, type of report, and complainant (if any)
2. Name and identification of the person writing the report
3. Office, agency, or business of origin
4. Report status—open, pending, supplemental, closing
5. Distribution—persons to whom the report is to be sent
6. Synopsis—a brief description of the case or investigation
7. Details of the report—a narrative, including all facts acquired and all *developed* leads
8. Conclusions and recommendations—this is the place for opinions and personal recommendations
9. Undeveloped leads
10. Enclosure list, including photographs, sketches, copies of documents, evidence receipts, computer disks

Writing Style

In an attempt to sound official, public safety and security personnel often adopt a writing style and use language that is elaborate, redundant, obscure, and full of jargon and legalese.

Clear, concise, simple, commonly used English vocabulary is best. Examples of jargon and wordy phrases and their concise, simple English counterparts include the following:

- Proceeded to the location (went to [specify location])
- Terminate (end)
- Approximately (about)
- Initiated (began)
- Related (said)
- Party (person)
- In view of the fact that (because)
- For the purpose of (to)
- Conducted an investigation (investigated)
- On an individual basis (individually)
- Unit (car)
- Went in pursuit of alleged perpetrator (ran after suspect)
- Deceased (dead)
- Maintained visual contact (watched)

Studies have demonstrated that word and sentence length determine readability and understanding. Long words and sentences tend to increase the need for a higher reading level. In report writing, the author of the report should present accurate information using brevity and clarity as guides to readability. Writers should avoid using words of more than two syllables, and sentences should not exceed ten to fifteen words.

Correct spelling and word usage and proper punctuation and capitalization are essential elements of good report writing. Mistakes in these areas may lead the reader to believe that the writer is undereducated, poorly trained, or careless. The writer should not rely on computer spell-check programs. The following are examples of inappropriate words that would not be identified with a spell-checker software program:

- She was identified as a drug *attic.*
- It was a *miner* incident.
- He injured his left *feet.*
- The item was found in the car's *truck.*
- The suspect fell into a *whole.*

Reports should be written to express a thought, not impress the reader. The language used in normal conversation should be the language used in the report. The vocabulary and style used should approximate what and how the writer would communicate if telling a story or explaining what happened during an incident. Report writers should not attempt to replicate the writing style of someone else. If the author of the report is required to testify in court, the language used in the report should be the same as is presented orally on the witness stand. First person, singular is recommended for describing what the report writer did, saw, or experienced. It seems more natural to expect that *I* did something rather than *Officer Smith* did something.

REFERENCES

Adams, T. F. 1998. *Police field operations.* Upper Saddle River, N.J.: Prentice-Hall.

Brislin, R. F., B. Cirignano, and C. Varner. 1991. *Effective report writing for the security officer.* Akron: Professional Education Services.

Hess, K. M. 1997. The ABCs of report writing. *Security Management* 41, No. 12 (December): 123–124.

Parr, L. A. 1991. *Police report writing essentials.* Placerville, Calif.: Custom Publishing.

Chapter 17

Professional Career Education

The need for highly educated and trained public safety and security personnel was recognized as early as 1931 when the United States government issued the Wickersham Commission report. Because of increasing national concern over crime, President Herbert Hoover appointed congressman George Wickersham to head a commission given the responsibility of investigating the nature and scope of crime and the administration of justice in the United States. To improve the quality of law enforcement personnel, the commission recommended that all police officers be required to possess a college degree.

In 1967, the President's Commission on Law Observance and Administration of Justice concurred with the position of the Wickersham Commission and recommended that entry-level police officers be required to hold a college degree. Congress responded to the President's Crime Commission report by passing the Omnibus Crime Control Act of 1968. The act provided funding sources for college education programs for public safety personnel and state training programs for police officers.

In 1976, the National Advisory Commission on Criminal Justice Standards and Goals recommended increased levels of training for security personnel in its task force report on private security. Similar education and training recommendations were developed and exist today for judicial, corrections, fire service, and environmental safety personnel.

Since the 1960s, college-level educational programs as well as preservice and in-service training programs for public safety and security personnel have proliferated. However, a debate over the appropriate focus of these education and training programs continues to exist in academe, particularly between traditional college degree programs and training providers. Some argue that *training* and *education* are not synonymous because training focuses on the development of specific job skills whereas the mission of education is to provide a broad-based understanding of the world.

The solution may be in the development of a complementary relationship between training and education. Colleges and universities could be encouraged to provide instruction focused on the development of nontechnical competencies, and preservice and in-service training programs could be encouraged to focus on technical, job-related skills. As an alternative, education and training programs could be merged or blended to form a program that provides instruction in general education as well as job-specific tasks.

CAREER EDUCATION

The terms *education* and *training* often connote distinctly different meanings and approaches to learning. Education is often referred to as broad-based development of general knowledge. Training, on the other hand, refers to the development of specific skills or competencies related to tasks performed by an individual. When addressing human resource development, the author suggests that training and education be merged and viewed from a global perspective. The emphasis in occupational education should be on professional development. Thus any learning activity designed to prepare an individual for, or improve performance in an occupation may be referred to as *professional career education.*

A professional career education model should focus on the development of nontechnical and technical competencies. Competence in leadership, human relations, written and oral communication, critical thinking, and problem solving are just as important as driving skills and dexterity in handling equipment. People are an organization's greatest asset. The success of an organization depends on its personnel. What employees know, how they perform, the values they possess, and the judgment they exercise determine outcomes for any enterprise. To ensure high productivity, quality performance and deference to an ethical standard, professional career education must be the top priority.

LEARNING CONCEPTS

Pedagogy is defined as the art and science of teaching, especially as it relates to instructional methods. The pedagogic style for teaching children and teenagers, however, is not appropriate for adults. Differences with respect to experience, education, and level of motivation necessitate a different approach in adult learning. To address these differences, Malcolm Knowles developed a philosophy and set of principles that are more consistent with adult learning needs. He called his new approach andragogy. According to Knowles (1970), andragogy, or the art and science of helping adults learn, embodies five key principles, as follows:

1. The participant accepts the material presented on the basis of evidence, not blind faith. The participant must be aware of the credibility of the information and how it relates to the real world in which the person operates.
2. The adult learner is active (rather than passive) during the learning process. Participants contribute their thoughts and ideas and relate relevant personal experiences to the subject being taught.

3. Participants' individual needs must be addressed. Even though experience and education levels vary, an instructor who facilitates discussions well can provide a valuable learning experience for even the most knowledgeable person.
4. The participants evaluate themselves. As learning progresses, participants conduct internal self-assessments of their understanding of the material and how it relates to their personal situation.
5. Instructional methods that promote effective adult learning are used. Discussion, role playing, and the demonstration method of instruction provide an opportunity for participants to interact with one another and promote an effective learning environment.

Andragogy involves a learning process through which the student and the instructor assume responsibility for what, when, where, and how learning takes place and to whom the learning process is directed.

CURRICULUM DEVELOPMENT, IMPLEMENTATION, AND EVALUATION

Proper career education results in professional action. Proper educational preparation and training are vital to effective job performance and promote personal and professional growth. The ultimate goal of any occupation-based curriculum is to prepare individuals to perform well. Therefore career education programs to be effective must be performance based.

To meet the employment demands of the contemporary workplace, workers should be required to demonstrate real-world, integrated job skills. This, according to the U.S. Department of Labor Secretary's Commission on Achieving Necessary Skills (SCANS), requires a three-part foundation that includes basic skills (reading, writing, computation, listening, and speaking), creative thinking and problem-solving skills, and personal qualities associated with responsibility, self-management, and integrity. According to SCANS, workers of today and the future should be able to demonstrate ability in the following five competency groups:

- Resources—the ability to identify, organize, plan, and allocate resources
- Interpersonal—the ability to work well with others
- Information—the ability to acquire and use information
- Systems—the ability to understand complex relations
- Technology—the ability to work with a variety of technologies

Career education programs should be relevant to the workplace and promote critical thinking, problem solving, flexibility, teamwork, leadership, and communication. Federal legislation has funded programs designed to develop these competencies. Examples include the Vocational and Applied Technology

Education Act (VATEA) of 1990 and the School-to-Work Opportunities Act of 1994. This legislation funded training programs relevant to the workplace.

The process for developing and presenting curricula is similar to the common principles of administration discussed in Chapter 10. These common principles include planning, implementation, leadership, and evaluation. Planning begins with an occupational analysis. An occupational (job-task) analysis is critical to the success of a training program. The job-task information collected and analyzed becomes the foundation for workforce training curriculum development. The analysis should identify general skills, such as those articulated in the SCANS report, and specific job-related skills and desired employee qualities. In other words, as a result of the training, what should the trainees know and be able to do, and how should they think and act?

Attention must be given to psychomotor, cognitive, and affective skill development. Psychomotor skills are needed to perform functions that require manipulation of tools, such as weapons and fire apparatus. Cognitive skills are needed so the employee can perform knowledgeably. Knowing the law, for example, is vital to success in public safety and security occupations. Affective skills are needed to demonstrate desired values and attitudes consistent with those demanded of public servants and security personnel.

Once job-related competencies and human behaviors have been identified, the training program can be developed and implemented. Care must be exercised to obtain valid assessments of what the trainee has learned. Assessment tools (tests, demonstrations, presentations) should replicate the actual performance standards of the workplace and be measurable. With performance-based instruction, the ultimate goal of student-learner assessments (evaluations) is to determine whether the trainee can apply what has been learned. In other words, can the trainee perform the job tasks according to the standard identified through the occupational analysis?

INSTRUCTIONAL GOALS AND OBJECTIVES

An instructional goal is the learning outcome expected at the conclusion of an instructional process. These goals may be viewed as terminal objectives. Guidelines for developing instructional goals include the following:

1. Translate the job outcomes into educational outcomes by reorienting the statement to the thinking skill required and context in which the performance occurs.
2. Develop the outcomes around the essential functions or problems of the discipline or job area; try to focus on developing seven to ten outcomes.
3. Reflect the breadth of application students may face in specific job positions.
4. Include the personal interactions, communications, and basic skill requirements related to the performance.

5. Write the statements in such a way that they suggest their own importance for learning in relevant, authentic terms.

Instructional (enabling) objectives describe the skills and behaviors a learner is expected to exhibit to demonstrate competence in the field of study. Instructional objectives must be measurable (performance based) and enable the learner to achieve the instructional goal. Written tests, oral presentations, and practical demonstrations may be used to measure performance and progress toward meeting instructional goals. Instructional objectives should be developed according to the following guidelines:

1. Offer a balanced core of learning in each course.
2. Adopt the belief that in-depth study of a limited number of important topics will have a more lasting effect than a course that tries to cover many disconnected bits and pieces.
3. Design course outcomes to focus on results with multiple indicators (assessments) of performance.
4. Design authentic assessments that will encourage originality, insight, problem solving, and mastery of important information.
5. Design courses to ensure active involvement.
6. Avoid tracking plans that assign students to a particular level and deny some students the opportunity to acquire knowledge and skills to succeed at a high level.
7. Get students *doing* early in the course rather than studying all the principles and basics before performing.

Perhaps the most widely accepted approach to developing and classifying instructional objectives may be found in *Taxonomy of Educational Objectives* (Bloom, Englehart, Furst, Hill, and Krathwohl 1956). The taxonomy serves as a guide to specifying performance outcomes and provides a hierarchy of thinking processes that enable learners to develop an understanding of complex material. The taxonomy has six levels, as follows:

1. Knowledge. This is the simplest level and represents a mere recall of facts or other memorized information. Verbs most commonly used in knowledge level objectives include define, state, repeat, locate, name, and recognize.
   Example: At the completion of this course, the learner should be able to define the crime of burglary.
2. Comprehension. Slightly broader than the knowledge level, comprehension level performance standards require the learner to organize facts and select among available alternatives. Some verbs used in comprehension level objectives include describe, identify, discuss, estimate, and summarize.
   Example: At the completion of this course, the learner should be able to identify a situation in which a burglary may have occurred.

3. Application. At this level, a learner should be able to apply skills or information learned to new and different situations. Some verbs used in application level objectives include solve, illustrate, translate, and interpret.

Example: At the completion of this course, the learner should be able to solve a burglary case if presented with appropriate evidence.

4. Analysis. At this level, the learner should be able to classify and sort information. Some verbs used in the analysis level include differentiate, criticize, categorize, compare, and contrast.

Example: At the completion of this course, the learner should be able to differentiate burglary from robbery.

5. Synthesis. At the synthesis level, the learner must combine ideas from previous learning to create new concepts and information. Some verbs that characterize the synthesis level include create, design, develop, organize, compose, and construct.

Example: At the completion of this course, the learner should be able to create a burglary prevention program.

6. Evaluation. The highest level of the *Taxonomy*, evaluation requires the learner to make decisions and exercise judgment on the basis of previously known facts or opinions. Some verbs that characterize this level include evaluate, appraise, assess, prioritize, justify, and recommend.

Example: At the completion of this course, the learner should be able to evaluate the effectiveness of a burglary prevention program.

The program of instruction must be evaluated. Evaluation of the learner's progress and assessment of outcomes should be matched to the instructional objectives. Methods used to assess learner performance should replicate, as closely as possible, the actual performance standards in the workplace. Written tests should not be the only assessment tool. Projects, team activities, demonstrations, and simulations also help predict success in the actual work environment.

REFERENCES

Bloom, B., M. Englehart, E. Furst, W. Hill, and D. Krathwohl. 1956. *Taxonomy of educational objectives: The classification of educational goals. Handbook 1: Cognitive Domain.* New York: David McKay.

Foran, J. V., D. J. Pucell, R. T. Fruehling, and J. C. Johnson. 1992. *Effective curriculum planning: Performances, outcomes, and standards.* Eden Prairie, Minn.: Paradigm Publishing.

Knowles, M. S. 1970. *The modern practice of adult education: Andragogy versus pedagogy.* New York: Association Press.

National Advisory Commission on Criminal Justice Standards and Goals. 1976. *Report of the task force on private security.* Washington, D.C.: U.S. Government Printing Office.

Nicholson, L. G. 1997. *Instructor development training: A guide for security and law enforcement.* Boston: Butterworth-Heinemann.

Ortmeier, P. J. 1995. Educating law enforcement officers for community policing. *Police and Security News* 11, No. 4 (July/August): 46–47.

Ortmeier, P. J. 1995. Security management: A career education master plan. *California Security* 1, No. 8 (October-November): 8–9.

Ortmeier, P. J. 1996. Placement in employment. *The Cohort of San Diego State University.* 1 No. 5 (May): 1–2.

Ortmeier, P. J. 1996. Adding class to security. *Security Management* 40, No. 7 (July): 99–101.

Ortmeier, P. J. 1996. *Community policing leadership: A Delphi study to identify essential competencies.* Ann Arbor, Mich.: UMI Publishing.

Ortmeier, P. J. 1997. Leadership for community policing: Identifying essential officer competencies. *The Police Chief* 64, No. 10 (October): 88–91, 93.

Pike, R. W. 1992. *Creative training techniques handbook.* Minneapolis: Lakewood Publications.

President's Commission on Law Observance and Administration of Justice. 1967. *Task force report: Police.* Washington, D.C.: U.S. Government Printing Office.

Index